AMERICA IN RETREAT

Stephen Barber, one of Britain's best-known and most widely travelled foreign correspondents, is chief of the Daily Telegraph's Washington Bureau. He has the knack of always being at the centre of events. As a war reporter, he saw action from Alamein to Anzio, behind the lines in Greece and with partisans in Italy. He covered the Greek Civil War, the Palestinian troubles, operations in Kurdistan, Malaya, Kenya and Korea. He was in Hanoi to witness the French collapse in Indo-China, in Goa when India seized it, in India when the Chinese struck in the Himalayas, and in Dallas when President Kennedy was assassinated and Oswald shot.

He has been living in Washington, D.C., since 1963. Alongside his reputation as a foreign correspondent, he has built himself a name in the US as a lecturer. He is married, with one son.

The West takes for granted the strength and leadership of the US. But how soundly based are these assumptions?

Today in the US the symptoms of defeatism and withdrawal are rife. Stephen Barber, who has been observing and writing about the American scene for a generation, demonstrates here how fragile is America's will and ability to lead the free world. Neither history nor national character equip the US for this role into which she has drifted.

Today—suddenly and unexpectedly—we are awakening to the fact that the champion of the free world is suffering a crisis of self-confidence and purpose. This crisis is far from over. The road to recovery may be rough: right now America is growing increasingly ungovernable. The consequences for the rest of the world are vast.

Stephen Barber's personal, penetrating analysis is the first book-length study of the most important political phenomenon of the 1970's.

AMERICA
IN RETREAT

Stephen Barber

BARNES & NOBLE INC.

NEW YORK

First published 1970 by
Tom Stacey Ltd
28 Maiden Lane
London WC2E 7JP

Reprinted 1971

Printed in Great Britain by
Northumberland Press Ltd
Gateshead

CONTENTS

Preface by Tom Stacey

The need for long-term thinking has never been as great as in the present era—and that need will increase at an accelerating pace. Few of the really major problems in the world are in fact *seriously* entertained by the governments of democratic countries—problems such as population control, world food resources and (and here we come nearer the point) the preservation of human motive in a world of technological revolution.

It is this last factor that particularly applies to the United States. It is something that threatens not only the role of the United States as the principal champion of the West and the chief guardian of its liberties over the next generation, but also, in the longer term, the survival of our civilization as we know it.

I share Stephen Barber's impression of the situation in the United States at the start of the 1970s—of the two wings of articulate opinion and behaviour in society being touched with a kind of mania, and a large depressive lump in the middle. Both the wings are tending to gather emotional force at the present time, like magnetic opposites.

It is the so-called New Left that has made most of the running; and although this New Left by definition can never actually win—since its self-stated objectives are nihilistic and anarchistic and do not countenance anything in the nature of a concrete victory or achievement of any kind—this group may well yet so infect the whole of society as to bring about something very

7

close to the disintegration of the Christian-based, competitive, responsible North American society we have known. If society does not actually fall apart it may well induce so exaggerated a reaction on what one might call the Far Right, that the result may be no less significant for America and the rest of the world.

The extremes, of course, would not be alarming if it were not for the fact that the lumpen middle is at present without noticeable conviction or courage or hope. I sense little strength or direction in the mass of American society. It is very much a situation like that described in Yeats' ever more frequently quoted poem—one in which 'the best lack all conviction, while the worst are full of passionate intensity'.

This has not always been so. Up to the late 1950s, the United States sometimes seemed a little ridiculous to the rest of us because of its excitable over-protection of what it felt to be its ideals, against such hostile forces as Communism or any form of 'unAmericanism'. There was a presumption that the American dream, the American way of life, was not only desirable to the rest of mankind deprived of anything comparable, but that it was also exportable. That presumption belonged to the great majority of Americans. Progress was still a perfectly valid god. Everyone assumed that, if the malign conspiracy of Communism could be held in check, and such cataclysms as world wars could be avoided, progress was inevitable and (it went without saying) eagerly awaited by the whole of mankind.

It was on these premises that the US threw itself behind the so-called nationalist movements in the colonial world and pressured the European powers to disband their empires. The same convictions permitted President after President to devote enormous sums to aid throughout the world and to the support of non-Communist regimes. It was in part the inspirer of an attitude of responsibility towards a shattered Europe after 1945. Some of America's convictions may have been misplaced, as we would see them; but the convictions were there, and their intentions were fundamentally honourable. Moreover, the great mass of Americans, if obliged to, would have been able to equate those convictions with a general view of life which embraced much that Western civilization, and particularly the 'Protestant ethic', stood for.

Jack Kennedy, when he came to power in 1960, appeared to exemplify what was most adult and intelligent in the basic idealism that had been so carefully propagated in the United States by the Anglo-Saxon establishment ever since the great rush of immigration began at the end of the last century. In their determination to force a nation, whose collective loyalty and sense of service could be appealed to for the good of themselves and the world, the American leadership had built up a sense of patriotism and idealism that did not seem to many to be a reasonably stable constituent of the world scene. All this Kennedy inherited, and evidently hoped to transform into something livelier and more fashionable.

Today we can see how much all of this has decayed since those not-so-distant Kennedy days. Stephen Barber demonstrates, in particular, how fragile the historical foundations of US supremacy had always been.

One of the most significant aspects of the United States today is the absence of coherent leadership. I suspect that when a people finds itself without a leader of calibre, without someone who can inspire the majority to be greater than its individual members would have thought possible, it is because that nation does not want leadership, is incapable of responding to leadership.

(Conversely, of course, when a people is once again ready to accept a leader they will swiftly find one.)

President Nixon possesses that synthetic quality of a man reconstructed out of the parts of others. In office, Nixon has evinced little sense of purpose, and the American people as a whole are experiencing little or no feeling of leadership. Nixon's stamp on events is a lot less than that of Lyndon Johnson; and negligible compared to Kennedy. He has sometimes shown signs of a desire to retreat from the limelight. Seclusion is acceptable in a leader of supreme confidence: in a man who lacks it, withdrawal generates uncertainty.

It seems we must accept the fact that Nixon is not of the stuff to rally the dispirited centre of the American populace and to draw the two fast polarizing wings towards their centre. At this juncture in American history, this is a pretty serious matter.

Let us look at the hard reality of the United States over the next year or two. During this time, the people of America—the greatest nation on earth, champion of the free world, the most rich and honourable and democratic and enviable among all mankind (in their old view of themselves)—will find that they have lost a protracted war in which they have sacrificed some 40,000 of their young men, the first war they have ever lost, and against a piddling, coloured, Communist enemy of negligible wealth and technology. Two or three million young Americans, and—through them—half the families in the US, will have participated in this fiasco.

Now, in the midst of this Vietnam trauma, they will be witnessing their own youth at home—and more than their youth: an increasing swathe of middle-class, middle IQ society—exhibiting many of the classic symptoms of decadence. The message is there in daily reports of civil unrest, of conflict between the generations, hostility between the college-educated youth and 'blue collar' workers. The message is there in every publication, poster, pronouncement of the New Left pleading for escapism through ever more desperate sensuality, mindless violence against authority and inchoate protest. It is there in Negro militancy, student power and contempt for country.

Too many young people in America today are searching away from the light for identity and purpose. Over the past year or two, this search has grown more frenzied and will grow more frenzied as their predicament grows worse. We are only just beginning to perceive the reverse side of frenzy, which is despair.

Within it all, into a society living increasingly on credit, as Mr Barber shows, there emerges an economic recession that seems likely to deepen.

Let us turn for a moment to consider the precise nature of this predicament. Clearly a predicament must exist: it is no good those of us not involved in this surge of irrationality to dismiss it as negligible or a passing phase (because it will not prove to be so); nor as something which can be put right by application of discipline from the police. (In the long run the only valuable discipline is what one might call positive discipline: discipline demanded by some objective, by loyalty to a purpose or a talent.)

In my view the predicament consists, at its centre, of the virtually total exclusion of concrete challenge. The American young today all have enough money—unlike their parents who grew up in the Depression. The physical challenges are no longer available unless gone after in the most selfconscious manner. The frontier has gone. Alaska is a cold, grim dump. Most of the physic-

ally demanding sports are only for the professionals.
There is, of course, the Draft. But it is, on the whole,
the sub-college youth and the Negro who get drafted,
and anyway, since Vietnam is being lost, it is a discredited cause and has no longer any power to evoke
the higher emotions of loyalty and sacrifice to a cause
or an ideal.

There is today no sort of international crusade for
the young to participate in comparable to the World
War of their fathers. There is the Peace Corps, but the
Peace Corps volunteers can never amount to more than
a tiny fraction of American youth. The young no longer
have any moral barricades to storm. By and large, pro-
miscuity, drugs, long hair, pornography, obscene
language in print or from the platform, or freedom
from soap, are all accepted with a shrug or even
applause. Life to the young today is a life without any
sort of restraint, and is pervaded by a feeling of in-
adequacy, surfeit and incompleteness.

It is a condition which needs a definite mental effort
to envisage by those conditioned to accept certain
values, norms of behaviour and limits of conduct. As
a young person in big city America today you can keep
all your options open all the time. You can indulge
freely in any form of sensual experience. You can get
drunk, go on a 'trip', copulate on the campus, start
riot, grow your hair to your waist, leave home, im-
mobilize your university, threaten your tutor with
violence, burn your draft card, break windows or commit arson in the names of the spirits of Che Guevara
and Lumumba and Ho Chi Minh—all without raising
a ripple on the surface of society. Your parents will react with numb acceptance. Your professors will react
with guilt, woolly approval, or mute fear.

In the view of the great majority of the young, their

elders are unable to offer any valid motive for behaving otherwise. There was a significant moment in that skilfully written and acted movie, THE GRADUATE, in the middle of the cocktail party thrown by his smart middle-class parents to celebrate his graduation, when the young hero is taken aside by his father's best friend to be given—in a single portentous word—the secret of a successful life: 'Plastics!'

The luckless modern youth of the United States is in a dilemma. He cannot go hungry. He cannot see a way of testing his courage in an honourable cause; he cannot shock. And so, he must push his behaviour before him into infinite licence and disorder, clinging bravely if pathetically to a corrupted existentialism which, unknown to him, is destroying his instinctual motives for making anything of his life or even his fitness to combat the materialistic corruption endemic in the society he wishes to reform. That is to say—if I may define this type of existentialism—he is reducing his experience to the lowest denominator of physical sensation, to a level below that at which such motives as love between man and woman, loyalty to a group or a cause, or any sense of achievement in life, can operate.

It is only when the disorientated youth that I have described meets the night-sticks of the police that at last—and usually with deep relief and even some recrudescence of pride—he encounters some sort of an obstacle: something palpable to run up against and to hate. The police and National Guardsmen often behave ludicrously: they like to play at storm troopers and they carry their presumption of hostility to the point of inciting it. Even so, nothing that has happened so far—from the Democratic Convention of 1968 to the student deaths of May 1970—has been a Budapest or an Amritsar.

It is fashionable among the more elderly supporters of these manifestations to put forward the theory that the young people of today are full of idealism, and have a far more keenly developed sense of concern and responsibility than earlier generations did at a similar age. In my view that is nearly true, but not quite; and in not being quite true the reality is almost unrecognizeably distorted. The reality is that these people, insofar as they do give voice to any sort of ideal for their own society or to identification with those of the world's sufferers and underprivileged they somewhat randomly select, are not being primarily motivated from without, but in the first place are motivated by their own personal or collective neuroses.

The predicament of intelligent American youth is, in critical form, the predicament of the whole American population and indeed of our world-wide, technocratic civilization. There has been evidence a-plenty in Western Europe—the *evênements* in Paris, university rioting in Germany, industrial disorder in Italy, and in Britain rioting as an accepted means of protest and an indifferent or cynical electorate. Japan, also, has been showing the symptoms.

The key factors are altogether worse, more dispiriting, more threatening in the US than in Western Europe or Japan. The US's industrial and commercial and organizational establishment, which is largely unaware of its own power, is vaster, more ruthless and more 'faceless' than Europe's. In the US the alternatives to a hitherto exclusive materialism are more drastic. The 'power structure', to use the current pejorative term, is so intermeshed with a multiplicity of technological and distributive and marketing operations that it can offer no symbol of leadership. The significance of the individual employee is subdued or eliminated. Alongside this faceless establishment, the American is subjected to a mechanization that is no longer dominating the individual—as all machines have tended to do from the beginning—but for some time been subtly taking from him his own will and separating him decisively from what one might call his natural roots.

Again, Americans even more than the rest of Western mankind are caught up in an economic technique which has all but removed the individual's ability to make choices and decisions that mean anything. You can select your breakfast food. You can select the shape of your swimming pool, or, within the range of about half-a-dozen designs, the appearance of your motorcar—but that is the level at which most choices most keenly thought about in American society are made, once you have selected your mate.

In America particularly (it is true in Britain too) the average man is subjected to a manner of life as an office worker for a big organization—and this is what most young men must become—that is stealthily emasculating the male. The most valuable attribute of character for the great majority of the American middle-class today is the ability to get on snugly with one's fellow office workers, to depress aggressiveness and ambition, to hazard nothing, and to look forward to one's retirement.

The ordinary person is confronted by a surfeit of food, chattels and spurious opportunities (such as to sun himself at Acapulco, or become a hit at dinner parties by taking a course in conversation)—a surfeit that induces a perpetual sense of incompletion and opportunities missed.

At the same time he participates in a political system which is full of well-advertised but enormously inflated freedoms such as the four-yearly Presidential vote. Here

I would to some extent chime in with Dr Marcuse, the San Diego Professor of Philosophy whose diagnosis is often accurate, even if his remedies are indecipherable: he has called the democratic system as practised in the United States 'an instrument for absolving servitude'. There is something in it.

As Stephen Barber shows, cybernetics has joined the assault upon individual significance by taking over more and more of those tasks formerly within the control of individual human decision, reducing the significance of life. A factory hand released by technology to ever greater leisure (i.e. gentle self-indulgence attached to no scheme of life) may be content to spend large proportions of his life watching the 'boob toob', or go fishing. But a man educated towards an expectation of contributing to the sum of human achievement, whose existence is made superfluous by cybernetics, is beginning to look to a destiny of enforced leisure with tremors of hysteria.

All these factors account for the peculiar reluctance on the part of the older generation in the US to galvanize the young or direct them into constructive roles.

Recognizing more or less subconsciously the situation into which they are emerging, the New Left together with an increasing proportion of the young are reacting with a predictable ambivalence. On the one hand they are retreating from reality—notably through the use of drugs. On the other they are floundering about in the search for challenge and ideals, especially through an attempt to identify with the violence and disgust that belongs to the restive, unemployed Negro.

Drugs are an important constituent of the syndrome. The spread of drug-taking in the United States has become something to which authority more or less seems to have now capitulated. People no longer talk in terms of eliminating the drug menace but merely of the best methods of containing it. Out of a sense of confusion or despair, more and more influential sources of opinion —and I would include *Time* and *Life* magazines—have settled for the view that it is comparatively harmless for young people of high school age to fall into the drug habit. *Time*'s own statistics indicate that something like 6 million young Americans are now taking drugs, and that of these some 2 million are more or less dependent on them. Just how acceptable the taking of drugs has become among the American young is indicated by the number of Senators' and Assemblymen's children who have been picked up on drug charges.

It is significant how the recent *Time* survey of the drug problem finished: 'The goal probably should not be to eliminate drugs entirely, which is impossible, but to control them and diminish their allure by offering the only valid alternative—a life of challenge and fulfilment. That, as kids who have reached a mature understanding of drugs already know, can be a turn-on, and a better one.' (Note that reference to children drug-takers 'who have reached a mature understanding of drugs'. What dangerous bunk!)

For myself, I do not regard the colour question as central to the American dilemma. I appreciate that the deprived Negro, in his slummy ghetto, who is protesting his lot by violent talk or action, has become an heroic figure to many young whites: here at last, in their very midst, is a species with a whole range of manifest grievances, reacting with a more or less virile counter-challenge to the whole system. Yet I suspect this indentification to be shallow and passing. It is more to satisfy their own psychological needs that white liberals and youth have obliged the formerly passive Negro to exercise his right to feel equal. In fact, for some time now, three or four years at least, the non-violent methods of Negro self-assertion have become discredited; integration is no longer the goal of the Negro activists, but *apartheid*, and the sympathy of 'whitey', however altruistic, is widely scorned.

It should have been evident years ago that the whole Civil Rights movement must be self-defeating, except in terms of bland legislation. The more the Negro protested his right to identify with white society, to be part and parcel of that society, the more he must emphasize his Negro-ness, not only to the whites, but—more damagingly in the long run—to himself. Thus, as statutory barriers fell before the Civil Rights movement, the Negro felt not less but more different than ever before. A sense of equality is not easily bought by political or para-political action. Something much more subtle is involved.

It is a hard fact of human society that ethnic integration of any kind, between two groups of significant numbers, takes a very very long time to become a reality. For a weak minority, manifestly different in many ways from a self-contained and established majority, to secure its absorption into that white majority by sectarian protest could *only* become increasingly frenzied. It was an exercise that could never have got under way were it not for the readiness of a significant section of the majority to transfer its own neuroses on to the minority.

When we come to Vietnam we see the consequences of this malaise in the United States at their most vivid and immediate. The moratorium of October 1969 and the demonstrations of May 1970 against Nixon's intervention in Cambodia were interesting for two reasons. First because of the nature of the protest: what amounted to the substantial dislocation of a large part of this machine. And secondly because the protest repre-

sented an alliance between the hitherto notorious New
Left and a large swathe of mainstream middle-class
Americans.

In any case it now seems inevitable that by 1972 the
United States, for better or for worse, will have abandoned the South Vietnamese to their fate. By all the
evidence it must be assumed that within six months of
any effective American military presence being removed, the hammer and sickle will fly over Saigon.
Even if it does not, the magnitude of their failure will
will be inescapable to mainstream Americans. It would
be highly unrealistic to expect that the American nation
as a whole will escape the consequences of this failure.
National confidence will have been flawed right
through, the whole ethic of the American way of life
and its role in the rest of the world monstrously discredited.

It is unimportant whether or not the million or so
protestors are correct in their view that their countrymen should quit Vietnam. *They* certainly don't know
how right or wrong they will prove to be. Eisenhower's
old domino theory is scarcely less or more valid today
than it was a decade or so ago. By the record so far
there is not much reason to expect that any less
slaughter or misery will follow a precipitate American
withdrawal than has been taking place to date. Certainly nothing has happened since Americans began
fighting in Vietnam to suggest a change in the character
of Communism. The point is not whether the protestors
are right or wrong in their view, but that they should
have chosen, in such enormous numbers, to have put on
this tell-tale performance without any purpose more
coherent than indulgence in a pervasive self-disgust.

In an interview published in October 1969 Walter
Lippmann made the comment that 'derelicts from pro-

gress', as he called them, were not an unusual phenomenon in the history of the great revolutions (I suppose he
was referring to our current technological revolution).
But what surely *is* unusual is that such 'derelicts from
progress' should set the intellectual tone for the majority. My own distinct impression of the United States at
the moment is that this is what is taking place.

I am personally convinced that the disillusionment
and dismay that we are seeing in the United States is
not a surface phenomenon. During the remainder of
Nixon's administration and possibly for most of the
coming decade, we may see the process continuing and
government becoming more and more difficult. A
faltering economy is bound to contribute to this process.
In this coming period, the attention of Washington
will inevitably be drawn inwards. America's preoccupations will no longer be in a world context but a national
one.

It is probable, indeed likely, that the forces of reaction to the trends I have been describing will super-
vene. Stephen Barber vividly illustrates the portents.
Whichever trend prevails, we in Western Europe, and
not least in Britain, cannot on current evidence any
longer take for granted America's role as chief guardian
of the free world and as the spearhead—as it were—of
our civilization. The defence cut-backs that began
in 1969 will continue ... and accelerate.

One effect of what is happening in the United States,
therefore, must be that Europe will have to play a more
significant part not only in its own defence but in the
defence of the free world. Britain's casual abandonment
of defence commitments could not be worse timed.

On a more subtle level, it falls to Europe, and perhaps
most of all to us in Britain, to mark the trends in the

United States and so to gauge our own policies and the conduct of our own affairs as to avoid as far as possible the Gadarene slopes that are luring Americans in such great numbers.

At this level it means that those involved in the politics of our Western European community must safeguard at every turn human motive. The American philosopher/sociologist, Lewis Mumford, recently wrote that 'only by restoring primacy to the person—and to the experiences and disciplines that go into the making of persons—can the fatal imbalance be overcome'. The imbalance he was talking about was that selfsame imbalance between man as a human being and man as an extension of his own technological environment that I referred to above.

To us it also means that European co-operation must become a practical reality in as many fields as possible. It means that we must be prepared to re-think our systems of government, our very constitutions. It means that we must elevate the plane of our political thinking. We must reflect once more on our definitions of democracy and freedom. For too long Europe has complacently assumed the leadership and security of the Free World to be the responsibility of the US. The great value of Stephen Barber's important book is that it shows how careless and ill-founded that assumption has been and what little time we have to make amends.

Tom Stacey
July 1970

I

The Mood of Retreat

The United States of America enters the 1970s in a mood of retreat. The young giant of the West—the principal champion of its liberties and their guardian—is suddenly grown middle-aged, crotchety and fatigued. The optimism and the vigour so much admired and envied by older peoples has faded. The technological advances and vaunted managerial skills that others sought, often vainly, to emulate are no longer enough. They have fallen out of step. What is happening in America today is of profound importance to the rest of mankind. Not only, as Canada's Prime Minister, Pierre Trudeau put it, is it 'like being in bed with an elephant—alarming when it has nightmares', but also, by observing America's dilemma as technological pacemaker, we may contrive to avoid the same spiritual impasse. The contrast with the dawn of the 1960s is astonishing. America's age of Empire seems destined to be the shortest on record. That its people may have never consciously yearned for Caesar's purple is quite beside the point. Their leaders did. They greatly relished the paramountcy of Washington. It was a source of pride that the President in the White House was the most powerful man in the world.

The central urge of American opinion today is to pull back from the world. A spirit of isolationism is sweeping the nation that barely a decade ago felt it knew all the answers everywhere to everything: all problems could be solved, the impossible just took a little longer. Priding themselves in being what President Nixon has termed a 'can-do' people, they took on too much and went in over their heads. It will be a considerable time before they try it again.

They moved on from acceptance of the 'responsibilities of power', to quote the title of the book by General Maxwell Taylor, President Kennedy's Saigon proconsul, to feel ashamed of the 'arrogance of power'—as Senator Fulbright expressed the thought.

It is as if the spiritual and emotional experiences of Britain's imperial golden age had been compressed into a single generation since 1940. America has run the gamut from the overweaning paternalism of the guardianship concept of Empire—Lugard in Africa, Cromer in Egypt, Curzon in India—to the abjectly self-critical, not to say self-accusatory anti-colonialism of the Fabians, all in just about ten years.

Let it be firmly stated here that this is nothing for Europeans to gloat over. Nor need Lenin's heirs and disciples take comfort from it: they have fared much worse, after all, in pursuing not dissimilar materialistic ends by different means. The world is not going to be any better off when the Yank goes home. We may well be in for a ticklish period of readjustment before balance is restored.

Indochina was a blunder. This is scarcely a matter for debate in America today. What went wrong, whether the United States should have permitted itself to become embroiled, how the campaign might have been fought more effectively—all this can (and will) be discussed indefinitely. What is almost universally agreed amongst the congressmen and the public at large is that never again will US ground combat forces be fielded in any new theatre on the Asian mainland in any foreseeable circumstances.

The accumulating frustrations of Vietnam have produced a sense of futility and defeat. There was a time when this would have been stoutly denied: today it is publicly admitted. Senior White House advisers can state in confidential memoranda to the President that the war has been lost (for not being winnable); and when later (as inevitably happens in Washington) the relevant documents leak into the Press, the defeatist assessment raises no hackles. It is merely ignored as being too obvious to attract comment.

The impact of this on America's self-esteem and the morale of its military establishment has been severe. Vietnam has been a blow to the nation's imperial élite —they would reject the adjective, of course, as un-American—roughly equivalent to that dealt Britain's lords and masters by the bunglings of the Crimean and the Boer Wars, culminating in the carnage of 1914-18. Mercifully there has not been remotely comparable bloodshed as far as the US is concerned—the numbers of Asian dead have no place in the equation here. The staggering success amongst America's upper middle-class suburbanites of the BBC's *Forsyte Saga* television series has perhaps been symptomatic. They were clearly willing to identify with John Galsworthy's intensely materialistic but solid fictional family; somehow it struck a chord of nostalgia for days past when things were more stable and certain. I would not wonder if a revival of Noel Coward's *Cavalcade* were to be an instant Broadway hit with a similar audience. These Americans feel sorry for themselves. To reflect that others have been this way before may make it all the easier to bear.

Gloom and doom are fashionable in America now.

Never a people to under-react, the nation has come to the conclusion that it is sick. The dispute is not whether there is a sickness, but whether the source of it is within the body politic, and the degree to which it might be curable.

America's exciting technological advances, like those of our much earlier industrial revolution, were inevitably achieved with a prodigal disregard for ecology. It is a commonplace today that the great question for the 1970s is whether the nation should 'surrender or make peace with nature'. This was how President Nixon himself expressed it in his first State of the Union address. He called on his countrymen to 'make reparations for the damage we have done to our air, our land and our water'.

The ravages of the latter-day 'dark satanic mills' far surpass the wildest nightmares of William Blake. And it was—as in his time, too—sheer, heedless greed that created the situation. But in the United States today a point has been reached where serious scientists question whether mankind will survive into the 21st century. Some doubt whether America, which they blame for nearly half the pollution in the entire world, will be permitted by Nature to survive to 1980. Jeremiahs abound to predict that a divine providence should rectify the imbalance which makes 'each American child fifty times more burden on the environment than each Indian'. The words are those of Stanford University's ecologist, Paul Ehrlich.

It is against a background of *angst* and guilt and defeatism that one must observe the self-abandon of a people that ought to be the most contented in the world. Plain folk find themselves confused and angry. They are bitter at being led into such a seeming impasse by their supposed betters. They stick stars-and-stripes decals on their motor car windows and 'America —love it or leave it' labels on their bumpers. But the children of the upper classes, the intelligentsia and the power-élite have tended to 'turn off' and, in varying degrees, reject the so-called 'system'.

President Johnson was 'toppled by a mob'. This was the candid verdict of Daniel Patrick Moynihan, the Harvard sociologist whom Nixon picked as his chief adviser on urban problems, in a confidential report on the eve of the Republican's taking office. 'No matter that it was a mob of college professors, millionaires, flower children and Radcliffe girls,' he wrote. 'It was a mob that by early 1968 had effectively physically separated the Presidency from the people.' He went on to recall how it had got so bad that when Johnson wanted to attend the funeral of New York's Catholic Cardinal Spellman that year, he had to be 'slipped into St Patrick's Cathedral like a medieval felon seeking sanctuary'.

Moynihan noted that America had been stable for so long that the notion of instability did not instantly catch on; but he reminded Nixon also that the nation's origins are revolutionary and that this tradition 'gives an advantage to those who challenge authority rather than those who uphold it'. His advice to his chief was to avoid becoming personally identified with the war, which was lost, while concentrating on restoring confidence in the Presidency and government and maintaining economic stability. He stated with a rare and revealing candour that to achieve the former 'the blunt truth is that ending the draft would be the most important step you could take ... the children of the upper middle class will not be conscripted'. He urged that ending military conscription would de-fuse domestic turmoil. The draft was taking too many bright youngsters out of college whose potential services to the nation were too important to risk in the squalid jungles of Vietnam. One should never, he reminded, eat the seed corn.

What Moynihan was saying in effect was that it would have been permissible, if not wholly proper, to have gone on with the Vietnam campaign if it could have been done without upsetting the precious offspring of the affluent. He wasted no words on such outmoded concepts as duty or patriotism. After all, the strict legitimacy of the war was questionable—Congress never technically declared it—and the 'sense of institutions being legitimate,' he pointed out, 'is the glue that holds societies together. When it weakens, things come unstuck.'

Nixon has acted on Moynihan's advice. He was elected in 1968 to extricate the country from Vietnam. He has not yet ended conscription but is plainly moving to it as soon as he can. He has his constituency—the 'silent majority' of 'Middle America'—behind him for as long as he keeps withdrawing US troops from South-East Asia. There were some observers who foolishly predicted at the time he was nominated by the Republican Convention at Miami Beach that he would try to get peace in Vietnam by threatening to unleash America's nuclear power. This was, of course, just barely hinted at by him to placate residual 'hawk' sentiment that has almost entirely vanished since.

Moynihan was right, no doubt. But what is fascinating is that no exception was taken by any American of prominence, in or out of office, to his flagrantly cynical doctrine. It is more important that America's domestic fabric be preserved than that the nation complete an unpopular task to which it has set its hand. The Vietnam commitment is to be expeditiously cut back, regardless of the consequences to those who will suffer for it, in much the same way as a giant conglomerate corporation phases out a subsidiary that is ceasing to pay. The only proviso is the need to maintain a façade to disguise defeat. There has been no quarrel with the position that it is far more important to placate the children of the upper classes and the intellectual liberal establishment than to uphold national honour. The US is a nation that equates honour and glory with economic prosperity and achievement. The fact that America's economy was strained to the point of distortion by Vietnam was Johnson's essential error. For fear of losing the 1966 elections he neglected to raise taxes to pay for the war: inflation inevitably ensued.

Ironically, nothing has irritated the vocal critics of the war and America's loose-knit New Left more than the way that Nixon has coolly pinched their clothes from beside their favourite swimming hole. Finally persuaded that it is indeed his intention to get out of Vietnam, at least to the point where the war effort can be reduced to a level that is bearable in terms of American domestic political pressures, they are still not satisfied. They would prefer a public humiliation, the penitent's scourge, sackcloth and ashes. It outrages them that any thought should be given to fighting on at low cost, long term, employing largely professional US troops to sustain an Asian ally.

Nixon's foreign and defence policy cannot be described as a total rollback into Fortress America. But the new and deliberate accent on 'low profile' postures, on a new era of negotiation replacing that of confrontation as far as the Communist world is concerned, along with recognition that a 'multipolarity' now exists— meaning that neither super-power is seen commanding a monolithic bloc and new and independent forces are emerging—must be regarded as sophisticated justification for an 'orderly withdrawal to previously prepared positions'.

It is a mistake to overdo historical parallels, but it may be observed that as in Edwardian Britain after a not very popular campaign against the Boers there was considerable liberal opposition to the Dreadnought programme, so today in Washington there is deep controversy over defence spending. In particular, the wisdom is challenged of entering a new upward spiral in the Russo-American arms race by proceeding further with the development and deployment of multi-warhead missiles, anti-ballistic missile systems and yet other more advanced weaponry in space satellite destroyers. This is not only because these things are regarded as a terrible waste of money at a time when much else needs attention, but also because the prestige of the military, as such, has declined—again because of Vietnam.

Nixon has already ordered big cutbacks in defence spending, even as the New Left and others more moderate would have him reduce it more. The impact on the aircraft and space industries has been severe. Belatedly in the spring of 1970 it was realized that an early consequence of ending the Vietnam involvement, which has been costing the taxpayer $2,500 million a month for several years, was bound to be a sharp rise in unemployment. Several major firms have been hard hit and more will be. Add to this the effect of almost a million servicemen being turned loose on the labour market and the prospects of a recession look more like those of a slump.

As if all this was not cause enough for alarm—which it certainly is—America has an extra problem to contend with in race. Here, too, Nixon's advisers counselled a domestic equivalent to the low profile doctrine overseas. The black American, they argued, has made great strides forward during recent years towards full and equal rights under the law. But this had neither assuaged his hunger for more progress, nor had it been accomplished without arousing the ire of the black's traditional foe, the poor white. At the same time the Negro, taught since the mid-50s that he has an obligation to feel equal, has discovered that advances in integration have not cured persistent inferiority complex. Hence the activist Negro effort has swung towards a defiant assertion of negritude—'black is beautiful'—expressed with a militancy that invites white hostility. Result: The American Negro is economically unquestionably better off in 1970 than he was in 1960 but race relations are far worse.

The Nixon-Moynihan formula calls for dissolving the Negro lower class—the hard core, slum-dwelling, perennially unemployed who are habitually prone to violent crime—by upgrading it into a stable working class through job training programmes and the like. He pointed out correctly that black extremists use the existence of the ghetto jungle as a means of terrorizing the white majority as well as the Negro middle-class. The snag is that this is much easier said than done. Black-white bitterness is so high already that it takes little to set off explosions.

A disproportionate number of blacks fought in infantry squads in Vietnam. This may have been inevitable since the generally better-educated whites were needed for less exposed technical functions. But the effect has been twofold: black Americans deeply resent that far more of their blood, comparative to their numbers (11 per cent of the population) was shed in Vietnam than 'Whitey's', and more black Americans today not only have guns but have been trained to kill.

They can handle explosives, too. It can hardly be expected that hardened ex-soldiers returned from Asia will tolerate an unemployment ratio twice as high for the black as for the white when the post-Vietnam recession hits the nation. When the French finally quit Indochina in 1954, the defeated Expeditionary Force and its disgruntled colonels, muttering angrily about being stabbed in the back by politicians in Paris, could safely be side-tracked into Algeria. It provided a temporary safety valve. Serious American strategic analysts today fear that the US will in turn have its 'Algeria' in the ghettoes of the nation's decaying inner cities. The opening skirmishes have already begun.

What makes America's situation all the more perilous internally today is that it has grown too fast and may prove to be too big and complex to be governable. The instinct of Nixon and his fellow 'Middle Americans'— the great, soft, chewy centre of middle-class, middle-income, middle-brow, middle-aged 'silent majority'—is towards diminishing the overlordship of the Federal Government and devolving more power upon the States. This is favoured by conservatives, naturally, since it offers endless scope for prevarication on the implementation of social and other reforms that appear more attractive to theorists at a distance than to unreconstructed individualists in the sticks. Experience has shown that Washington's writ simply does not run when a recalcitrant local authority dislikes a programme. The alternative to devolution, concentration of power at the centre, is unlikely to work well either. The institutions of America's Federal Government have so proliferated with congressional and departmental committees and subcommittees as to become grossly cumbersome and perhaps eventually inoperable. The US Constitution, sacred in American eyes, was written for the governance of a handful of clubbable country gentlemen and professional men, not for two hundred million. The last purpose the framers had in mind was the creation of a structure to order the affairs of so huge a nation, let alone that it should fulfil an imperial role. That the great creaking engine works at all is a miracle, yet there are grave doubts about its chances of holding together much longer without major, radical and perilous overhaul.

The tradition of lawlessness is excused as an expression of the rugged frontier spirit that made America what it is, and inwardly absolved by a he-mannish attitude towards possession of personal firearms, but it is a continually disturbing factor in the worsening American sickness. The Congress can enact laws: the courts may uphold them. But verdicts can be appealed against for years and the entire US courts' system is clogged up with litigation to the point where, as an everyday instance, a man caught red-handed robbing a bank may be out on bail for 18 months or more. Criminal cases are tortuously delayed, but civil actions can be spun out longer still.

There is very little faith that Justice is even-handed. It can be quixotically quick or preposterously slow. Since lower court judges are elected, they are subject to obvious pressures. Result: the Law is not respected in the way it is in European countries. Corruption is rife. The police in general are not respected. Crime flourishes, often with their tacit connivance. It is accepted as a fact of life that it is dangerous to venture out alone after dark in most big cities. Since the chances of being punished for armed assault are less than one in twenty, the wonder is that there is not more of it.

On top of everything else, America now is plagued by a craze for drugs on the part of her young that has reached epidemic proportions. The commonest cause of death amongst New Yorkers between 20 and 24 is narcotics' overdose. Dr Stanley Yolles, director of the National Institute of Mental Health, estimates that between 12 and 20 million Americans use marijuana. Dr Judianne Densen-Gerber, a New York specialist, has reckoned that 100,000 teenagers were on heroin in that city alone in 1970. 'We should stop worrying about a war with Russia,' she said. 'Russia won't have to fight us. We are becoming so decadent we have no strength to resist!' And allowing for her angle of vision, there is much in what she said. America's drug scene is linked with Vietnam: thousands learnt their habit there. Drug addiction has become the biggest medical problem in the US Army. Marijuana, opium and heroin are readily obtained in South-East Asia and Customs' officers have complained that the Army Post Office itself has become a major conduit for illicit drug imports.

The nation having inherited a 'system' that seems so cumbersome, unfeeling and unresponsive to the restless spirits of a bored, frustrated and bewildered youth, it is hardly to be wondered that the rhetoric of today's militants becomes continuously shriller. This is no time for the bland to be leading the bland. Partly because its principal preoccupations are the war and the war-wounded economy, partly because its main support comes from an essentially selfish, self-righteous and uncomprehending middle-class, the Nixon Administration seems increasingly paralysed. Nixon himself prefers to concentrate on global issues—understandably since, however great, they are relatively simple. The result is that domestically an aroused and alienated university student movement, headed by some of the wildest young nihilists ever to blow themselves up on home-made bombs, are embarked on a series of theatrical guerilla raids on the citadels of the Establishment or its symbols. They claim that this is the only way they can protest against the system. No matter that the system is itself hog-tied : no matter that they have no clearcut proposals for a substitute. They despise what Dr Herbert Marcuse, their *guru* in La Jolla, California, has termed the 'repressive tolerance' of liberal democracy.

It would be a mistake to underrate the numbers or significance of this inchoate and angry element. It may well also have turned out to be an error on the part of the Nixon Administration to enlist its participation in a well-intentioned national propaganda drive against the pollution of the environment. This seemed to be a good idea—to harness the idealism of youth to a common cause for all members of society to support. But rapidly it developed that the extremists had more extensive plans. They intended to turn the great campaign against the rape of mother earth into one which would focus direct attacks on industrial polluters, giant corporations, the bastions of capitalism, exploiters of the people, class enemies. In short, what was to have been a pepped up, Boy Scouts' Good Deed For the Day operation, was transformed and politicized into something much bigger. The US Government, as the biggest polluter of all, what with its napalm and poison gas and H-bombs, found itself transformed from huntsman into fox.

A portent of things to come occurred when, by way of expressing indignation at the sentencing of the Chicago Seven—the ringleaders of the anti-Vietnam war rallies during the Democratic Convention of 1968— students at Santa Barbara's Isla Vista campus of the University of California burned down a bank. A couple of days of sporadic rioting followed. But what concerned the authorities most was that they could be taken by surprise. Hitherto Isla Vista students had been regarded as somewhat apolitical hedonists. The firemen and police were even more shocked and appalled by the spectacle of semi-nude and bearded youngsters dancing around the flames of the bank and heaping money into the blaze instead of stealing it. This gesture of sacreligious contempt was deeply disconcerting.

Symbolism is all, as the militants perceive it. Another California university group in 1970 solemnly organized a ceremonial funeral for a brand new motor car. They dug a grave for it, having found it guilty of the sin of environmental pollution, 'executed' it and pronounced it 'dead'. The car, which had never been driven, was then heaved into its resting place and earth shovelled over it. A spirited wake was then held. To mar the jollification, a number of indignant Black Panthers arrived to protest that the odiously well-to-do white anti-pollutionists should not have wasted good money on buying a car to destroy it. They should have given the money to them for the Panthers' legal defence fund. Whereupon, without more ado, the revellers held a hasty whip round and came up with the car's purchase price all over again and gave it to their critics.

For an American to bury a car is like Hannibal burying his elephant, Cortés his horse or primitive Man the wheel. Nothing could symbolize the American way of life more appropriately than the modern car; economically, culturally and spiritually. To desecrate a new car is almost as disturbing an offence in the eyes of Middle Americans as burning the Stars and Stripes. This is, of course, why the youthful ecologists did it. They were not just demonstrating against the automotive age but against country itself.

It requires not great perspicacity, I feel, to predict where all this is surely leading. The New Left can be counted on to develop increasingly outrageous methods of goading Nixon's 'silent majority'. In its ranks are undoubtedly some of the brightest and most gifted youngsters in the nation. Many are the Establishment's own. But as tempers rise the impulse will be overwhelming to crack down with more repressive police measures. Riot squads will get bigger and bigger. So will the clashes. Polarization into 'we' and 'they' will harden. Dialogue will cease.

As economic tensions mount and the season comes round again for new Trades Union contract negotiations in key industries, which is liable to mean strikes and lock-outs, the prospect is for violence on the labour front, too. And lay-offs will spark trouble on the racial scene as blacks and whites vie for jobs.

If Hanoi should now decide to complicate Nixon's and America's problems by making it difficult for significantly more US troops to withdraw from Indochina without loss of face, then the clouds on the horizon will darken further. The North Vietnamese can outflank the South by moving in on Laos and Cambodia and challenging Thailand. America will stand revealed as a paper tiger—or have to widen the war. Nixon would be faced with an agonizing choice. The Congress has already tied his hands when, in passing the 1971 military budget, a rider was tacked on to the appropriation bill that bars funds for any deployment of American ground forces in Laos or Thailand. Had his Cambodian move been foreseen at the time, doubtless Senators would similarly have blocked it in advance. This may provide justification for him to do nothing in either country, but it will make it much harder to persuade President Thieu that he can get along with fewer US troops, as he must be if Nixon is to avoid going the way of Johnson.

This, then, is the basis for a sad scenario.

The hippie revolutionaries, as likely as not high on pot that is in itself an ingredient of the protest cult, will storm and rave. They will carry out more bomb plots—several have occurred already in 1970—and get themselves 'busted' in all kinds of deliberately provocative demonstrations. They have found violence exciting. They make decorative martyrs. The militant blacks will act similarly, sometimes in unison but often separately—the Panthers, for example, eschew what they call 'Custerism', meaning futile Last Stands where the defenders are wiped out to a man.

Then, and inexorably, reaction will set it. It has indeed begun. The New Left activists will not only collide with the official forces of Law and Order but also with white extremist vigilante groups. The nucleus of armed, far-right, super-patriot forces, such as the Minutemen, already exist. It may be safely anticipated that their ranks will be swollen by returning ex-servicemen from Vietnam—many of them poor whites of working class origins who are inclined to detest the draft-card-burning collegiate young with added bitterness for dodging the war they bled in. There is ample human material for the formation of Storm Troopers—and plenty of far-right, ultra-conservative millionaire money to fund them.

When the chips are down, there is no question today but the Right is much stronger than the Left in America. In a time of high crisis there is often a tendency to look for some authoritarian figure to lead—for 'a man on horseback'. It could well be that Nixon is the last ditch defender of the nation's liberals. His erstwhile Democrat opponents are in miserable disarray. He is certainly far more vulnerable to the Right than the Left. And America's Right is strongly isolationist, it must be emphasized, which means that if Nixon fails the odds are on a full retreat into Fortress America.

America is in crisis today on several fronts at once. It has to do with a growing loss of confidence and a sense of helplessness about the inability of Government, both at the Federal and local level, to cope with the problems of the times. What, after all, is one to say of a leadership class that, having led the nation into a Vietnam, then falls into an orgy of self-criticism and back-biting over being unable to find a way out? One by one most of the syndicated newspaper pundits who flew bravely with the hawks have come to earth—excepting only that pathetic diehard, Joseph Alsop, who lately began to adopt the mannerisms of Winston Churchill ... as if that might somehow save the day. For ordinary folk, the question keeps coming back: how did so many clever chiefs and elders get America into such a fix?

It is this, the erosion of confidence in the wisdom of rulers by the ruled, that must have alarming consequences. That such an essentially colourless, if grindingly hard-working lawyer-politician as Richard Milhouse Nixon should represent to many of his countrymen today the last, best hope is surely disturbing. It means—and he himself often seems readily to admit as much—that the bulk of Americans have had their fill of high adventure and lofty purpose and would rather be bored, boring, comfortable and commonplace. 'America may be the first country to turn fascist democratically,' William Shirer, chronicler of the *Rise and Fall of the Third Reich* and the *Collapse of the Third Republic*, wrote recently. The unnerving thing about this statement was that it was scarcely considered provocative.

America has overstrained herself. She remains vastly rich and powerful. But not in spirit. Time alone will show whether this is to be a permanent or merely a temporary condition. But, as Tacitus wrote of the reign of Galba, 'we now enter on the history of a period rich in disaster, gloomy in wars, rent by sedition and savage in its very hours of peace.'

2

The Nixon Doctrine

'That's one small step for man—one giant leap for mankind!'

The awe of Neil Armstrong, the Apollo astronaut, at being the first earthling to set foot upon the moon was movingly genuine. It was a thrilling moment for the American and for millions of his countrymen and others around the world who shared it, peering into the fuzziness of their television screens. The United States had 'won' the moon race against the Russians. The late President John Kennedy's goal of a manned lunar touchdown by the end of the decade of the 1960s had been achieved. The moon exploit was inspired by Kennedy's yearning to 'get the country moving again' following the slumbrous Eisenhower years. It was a sort of holy grail for the knights of his Camelot to pursue. Letting the Soviets make the running would have amounted to admitting the United States was 'second-rate'. Kennedy's decision in May 1961 to climb this space Everest was motivated by a determination to get even with the Russians, who had stolen a lead with Sputnik, and recover prestige which had further been dented by the Central Intelligence Agency's ill-fated attempt to overthrow Fidel Castro's Cuban Communists at the Bay of Pigs.

The spacemen were properly accorded the triumphs due the courageous upon their return by their countrymen, just as the Romans fêted their successful generals

back from outer Gaul. But each welcome home (Apollo
XIII not excepted) seems doomed to be less enthusiastically applauded than the last. Objections are increasingly
heard if the latest live TV transmission from space in-
terferes with the ball game. Just as the Romans may
well have felt about the news from Gaul, so Americans
have become about the moon: there are less expensive
and a lot more amusing circuses at the Colosseum. And
there is no question but that this feeling coincides with
a distinct falling away in interest in the realities and
responsibilities of world power.

While it can hardly have been intentional—although
future historians may deem it to have been predictable
—it seems somehow fitting that the culmination of
America's $24,000 million affair in space was to serve as
the curtain-raiser for the enunciation of the Nixon doctrine of disengagement in the officers' club of the US
Strategic Air Force base on Guam only a few hours
after the Apollo XI trio, their mission accomplished,
made the Pacific splashdown.

The 1960s indeed saw the Americans conquer the
moon, but the 1960s also saw their spirits crack under
the burdens of world leadership. The Imperium waxed
and waned: the briefest ever recorded. It may well be
argued that the role was never sought, that they had
greatness thrust upon them, that pro-consular attitudes
warred constantly with earnest missionary zeal in the
breasts of overseas administrators reared as anti-colonial-
ists in infancy. They did not want to be the world's
policemen, they insisted with sincerity: events compelled them to be against their will. (This argument
has, of course, been used by others in the past, including the British, and the French and Belgians with their
mission civilisatrice.)

The moon victory served handily to distract from an

Asian retreat for US arms. At Guam, in the immediate after-glow of the space spectacular, Nixon served notice that from there on, America intended to withdraw from the outer limits of Empire in the Western Pacific just as soon as the Vietnam conflict could be conveniently disposed of without too much loss of face. It was soon to become evident that the same doctrine is to apply in Europe as well.

After Vietnam, there are to be no more such adventures on the Asian mainland. Never again will 600,000 American soldiers, sailors and airmen find themselves tied up in a frustrating and seemingly endless and unwinnable war costing $2,500 million a month to prevent a tin-pot country going Communist. In future, it is to be up to friends and allies to save themselves in event of armed subversion, be it internally or externally directed. Only if a direct threat by nuclear power is involved can the US be counted on to move. In certain circumstances, and according to a coolly calculated assessment of American interests involved, it is still conceivable that US *matériel* and military advisers, counter-insurgency specialists and the like, may be forthcoming to help friends or allies in time of trouble. But as a general rule, the US intends taking a back seat in existing alliances and is decidedly unlikely to get involved in any new ones.

The Nixon Doctrine lays down that American presence in the Pacific shall be 'low profile' or 'hull down over the horizon'. That is to say, it shall be confined to naval and air forces almost exclusively. The US is in the Pacific by virtue of geography. It cannot, therefore, escape from the region completely—nor is that desired. Washington would hope that the nations of the area would, in due course, and on their own, think well of entering into collective defence arrangements—prefer-

ably with the US playing a very minor role, if not excluded. The Nixon Administration would be only too
delighted if the Japanese would see their way to playing
a leading part in such a security system, although all
the signs are that Japan is determined not to acquire
the label of 'the Ugly Asian'—even if it is not entirely
content to go on prospering mightily simply as 'the
Quiet Asian'. Tokyo's bankers fully expect to replace
America's as the paramount economic force in non-
Communist Asia during the 1970s and they say so:
they have no intention of slowing themselves down
with excessive military burdens.

Nixon made these intentions clear to those of us who
accompanied him on his round-the-world tour in July
1969 the night before he reached the Philippines, his
first port of call. It took some time for the US to grasp
the idea. This was partly because of the continuing
moonglow mood, but also because most commentators
either found it hard to square it with the Administration's continuing support for the Thieu regime in Saigon. The few remaining hawks still believed the war
could be won: the doves wanted instant withdrawal
and nothing less would unruffle them; those in between
were lulled by Nixon's careful, if purely formal, emphasis on keeping faith with existing commitments into
thinking nothing had really changed.

The Filipinos seized the point quickly enough. They
lost little time extricating their own contingent of en-
gineer troops from Vietnam and started probing for
business with Russia's Eastern European satellites. The
Thais, as Asia's perennial Vicars of Bray, likewise displayed a new and sudden interest in Iron Curtain trade
possibilities. The Nationalist Chinese in Formosa became understandably anxious. And in Vietnam, the
realization swiftly dawned that Nixon's decision to

withdraw troops as fast as Saigon's forces could be pressured into taking over the main burden of the fighting was irreversible: it was a case of sink or swim. The word was out: either the Americans no longer believed in the old domino theory—that if one country fell to the Communists, the one next door would topple next, or if they did believe it, such a sequence might no longer seem to them so tragic after all.

The plain fact was that a new and flexible policy doctrine had taken shape. It was to be Vietnam for the Vietnamese: Asia for the Asians and—in a more gingerly fashion—Europe for the Europeans.

It requires no great prophetic gifts to forecast a shrinking in American policy from now on. Short of a major catastrophe, there will be a steady retreat of US power and a deliberate down-grading of Washington's function as the leader of the Western alliance. That the nation will remain the richest on earth is hoped for, but no longer regarded as absolutely inevitable. There are respectable American economic prophets who already forecast that Japan will actually overtake the US in output-per-capita within 20 years—and a few predict sooner than that.

There can be no doubt that although the Nixon Administration has repeatedly reiterated pledges to maintain US troops strength committed to the North Atlantic Treaty Organization at the current level until mid-1971, cuts will be coming thereafter. The pressure in Congress is building up rapidly. It would have peaked earlier had it not been for the Soviet action in Czechoslovakia in 1968. That there is unlikely to be a total pull-out for some time to come is due to the fear that it would result in a clamour in West Germany for bigger defence forces, which in turn would provoke the Russians dangerously. If a genuinely workable deal could be arrived at for a balanced reduction of NATO and Warsaw Pact forces nobody would be happier than the Americans today. Without it, we must look forward to proposals whereby the European partners will be required to contribute more towards the support costs of the US component of the alliance. We shall also hear much about how the huge, new C5A Galaxy troop-carrier plane can airlift a complete battalion 6,000 miles in an emergency, permitting forces earmarked for NATO to be home-based and thus saving foreign exchange.

Nixon is in favour of an all-volunteer army. Military experts say this can be achieved within acceptable budgetary limits only if America's forces are reduced by over one-third to a total of about 2,000,000. It is then argued that such a force level would be inadequate to meet the nation's military commitments to some 43 allies around the world. This means revised commitments.

The trend is moving rapidly towards something akin to, but not exactly the same as, the old pre-war isolationism. America today has too much invested overseas and too many interests to protect to permit a return to the pre-war stance. Replacing it is a concept known as continentalism. This would have American power abroad confined to token garrisons backed by naval and air forces. It is easy to see that in short order this would result in the construction of a Fortress America, if under some other name, bristling with nuclear missiles and anti-missile systems. It would be more economical, certainly, since already both the super-powers possess vast 'overkill' capacity; but it would mean that the US would have less and less military flexibility to deal with anything other than total holocaust.

There is no single, simple explanation for this development.

Vietnam—the frustrations of a war that has cost 40,000 lives to no instantly discernable effect—is surely a major factor. The depth and fervour of pacifist opposition has led to a serious re-examination of America's ability to carry on operations of this type. It has certainly resulted in grave doubts about the use of US conventional military power in settling political conflicts. More than that, it has raised more than a suspicion that the nation's leadership is incompetent and even that it has somehow betrayed its assumed ideals and purposes. It should, however, be noted that these doubts and suspicions did not crop up at the outset of the involvement but only when the children of the affluent began to receive their call-up papers.

The impact of Vietnam on American morale is bound to be considerable if only because the Vietnam setback has come to a generation which had grown up with and become accustomed to the overwhelming rightness of its might and the general superiority of everything about the US. The Victorian British had a similar conceit over a longer period. The Americans, as a younger and less than stable people, are short-range crusaders. They now feel they have tried to do too much for too many and are surrounded by ingrates, besides. Moreover, as they look about them at their shabby, run-down city centres, soaring crime rate, sharpening racial conflict, the alarming alienation of what should surely be the brightest and best of the educated youth of the nation; as they watch rising prices and falling profits, tight money and high interest rates, budget cuts and short-time working in industry, they are entitled to be more than a trifle glum.

A certain type of Englishman, necessarily beyond

middle years today, is apt to comfort himself for the passing of imperial grandeurs with the reflection that, in Kennedy's phrase, 'the torch has been passed to a new generation of Americans'. These people sometimes carry fantasy further by dreaming of some closer Anglo-American relationship—even an outright union. Such an arrangement would, under any equitable terms, provide the more homogeneous British with a voting bloc in Congress that no equivalent American grouping could compete with. This, plainly, would not be tolerated. But the wistful thought persists—and hence the sadness of these very nostalgics on awakening to the realities. I recall one such, who, upon observing the Marines' Band at the White House trumpeting 'Hail to the Chief!' from the South Balcony during a British Prime Minister's visit, said pensively, 'Oh dear. It really ought to be the other way round. So much more *our* thing!' The same man, present in Kuala Lumpur some months later, found it 'unbearably mournful' to see Lyndon Johnson lay a wreath on the brand-new cenotaph to the fallen of Malaysia's anti-Communist struggle—a memorial innocent of any hint of the part played by British troops. But if melancholy, he also found it consoling that the Texan was playing Caesar. Today, of course, he feels all the more indignant that the Americans are so eager to surrender the role Johnson had assumed.

Ever since Rudyard Kipling wrote his poem 'The White Man's Burden' as an inspiration to his American wife's countrymen after Theodore Roosevelt's 'bully little war' with Spain, there have been Britons and Americans sharing the basic misconception about how the United States could and should be counted on to bear that burden. It was a basic error to imagine America must always bear it. The beguiling conceit of the 'special relationship', which Sir Winston Churchill entertained, or of being 'the Greeks to the new Romans', as Harold Macmillan's image ran, was understandable since both men had American mothers. But in others, and not only Britons but West Europeans of all kinds, the idea of a *Pax Americana* neatly succeeding a *Pax Britannica* is both fallacious and dangerously debilitating.

So far as America's allies are concerned—in Western Europe as well as in Asia—the writing on the wall is now very clear. Since 1945 half the world has allowed itself to accept, gladly at first and then often grumblingly, Washington's leadership. US military and economic aid has been taken for granted by scores of nations. In many cases it has not only been expected but regarded as a kind of right—a peculiar form of tribute due the poor from the prosperous. This cannot —and will not—go on.

Today the man in the White House is one who was already highly sceptical about such alliances as the South-East Asian Treaty Organization before he ran for the Presidency. Once in office, of course, he must pay a certain lip service to them. He is on record as being staunchly in favour of the North Atlantic Treaty —and in this case is doubtless more sincere. But it is no secret that he and his Administration chiefs feel strongly that America has borne an unfair share of the burden of mutual defence, and that the time has come for allies who have grown increasingly prosperous and strong themselves in recent years to start doing more for the common cause. Congressional opinion, which reflects even more directly that of the American public at large, is still more emphatic on the subject.

It should have surely been obvious that the time had to come when this would be so. Yet it seems to have caught more than a few of America's partners by surprise. Having based their defensive posture, particularly in the West, on a confidence bordering on total certainty that the US could be relied to stand firm if ever it came to a showdown, they neglected the study of alternatives.

Given the awesome realities of nuclear weapons and their destructiveness, what European President, Premier or Defence Minister today could dare go to his people, hand on heart, to say they can absolutely rely on America's springing to their aid in the event of Russia's invading their territory? It is hardly to be expected that Moscow would be so foolish as to risk a frontal engagement: penetration by subversion, the fomenting of internal revolution, is clearly the more effective method —and there is no way in which a nuclear warhead can cope with that.

More than a decade ago, the US Strategic Air Command's role—when General Lauris Norstad was NATO supremo—was that of the terrible, swift sword: the great deterrent. It was accepted dogma that if Russia moved against the West, the President of the US would 'mash the red button'—unleash the B52s and the nuclear-tipped rockets from their underground silos. But now all this is regarded as nonsense. It is recognized that no American leader responsible to his countrymen would seriously contemplate risking Chicago for the sake of Copenhagen. Short of a 100 per cent effective pre-emptive strike, it is agreed by all the experts nowadays that any war involving the super-powers would swiftly escalate into a maniacal trade-off of entire cities before the first day was out. But the moment there is any doubt that responses are automatic and pre-set— hit Copenhagen and we 'take out' Kiev; you flatten Chicago, or go for London, we annihilate Leningrad—

and the entire deterrent concept collapses.

The US today is developing a weapons system in competition with Russia's that promises to set off an upward spiral in defence spending of prodigious dimensions that will wind up at a new plateau of mutual terror, unless some agreement can be quickly reached to slow the process down. Quite apart from the fantastic costs involved, which are likely to cripple the economies of both participants in this sophisticated contest, the size and complexity of these new armaments are such as to remove them from consideration by the junior partners of either. Medium powers like Britain and France can aspire to nuclear sufficiency. A strong case can still be made for possessing one's own private deterrent, but they are simply *hors de concours* when it comes to MIRVs and ABM's, SABMIS, ULMS, orbiting spy satellites, space interceptors and so forth.

In short, it is impossible for America's military planners to integrate their strategic policies with those of relative midgets—or so they must feel. They live in another world. While they are too polite to express the thought for public consumption, it is inevitable that they see nuclear war as something that would be conducted from fortress to fortress: the peasantry who live in the marches are no longer relevant.

Concentration of ever-increasingly burdensome super-weapons has a further effect on alliances, too. If it is difficult to achieve guns and butter, it is still far more so to achieve guns, butter and a galaxy of new and far-out rockets, anti-missiles, anti-anti-missiles and so on. Legislators already groaning at the cost of these things to the taxpayer are bound to insist on budgetary cuts in other directions. The axe is almost certain to fall mainly on conventional forces rather than nuclear/ strategic ones because they are the most expensive and vulnerable item in the military budget. Pressure will mount irresistibly for troop cuts overseas—not least in Europe where their maintenance is a drain on US foreign exchange reserves.

Purely budgetary considerations thus combine with a national mood strongly inclined towards retrenchment. It must, therefore, be assumed that major reductions in US force levels assigned to NATO in Europe will take place in this decade of the '70s, coinciding with withdrawals from Asia. These moves will, of course, be suitably camouflaged with statesmanlike references to lessening tensions and interdependence, and how the world has moved from confrontation to negotiation. But this need fool no one. Wishful thinkers in the West may hope that America's 'nuclear umbrella' would be pledged to remain as a guarantee against atomic blackmail even after the last US soldier had boarded the final troopship for home. Yet such an offer is apt to be withdrawn the moment it looked like rain.

To be fair, US public figures have given their allies ample warning. Notice has been supplied in the form of Congressional resolutions calling for economies in the shape of major troop cuts overseas. Nixon has outlined at unprecedented length in his first so-called 'State of the World' message to the nation how he intends to pursue a 'low profile' foreign policy from now on. But perhaps the most significant single utterance that sums up the spirit in which America enters the 1970s was contained in a patriotic speech by Senator Richard Russell of Georgia, a highly respected elder who has long played a dominating role in US military affairs. He was taking part in 1969's anguished Senate deliberations on the anti-ballistic missile—deployment of which he strongly endorsed. He concluded with remarks that should surely be studied widely:

'If we have to start over again with another Adam and Eve,' he said, 'I want them to be Americans, and I want them on this continent and not in Europe.'

The statement has the virtue of total candour—and it is safe to say that the Senator's view is shared, although not expressed so baldly, by the Nixon Administration. It has to be. But it has seldom been deemed politic hitherto to declare in advance that a great nation's defence policy is to fight to the last ally even though that is its natural intent. It discourages loyalty.

The task of world leadership requires more than a taste for power or even power's possession. It demands the will to lead. And it is this peculiar and irreplaceable quality that the painful lessons of the 1960s have eroded in America.

3

The Uncertain Foundations
of World Leadership

The United States of America is today incomparably
the most powerful nation the world has ever seen. This
fact is so obvious it hardly needs saying. There are
many, especially in Europe, who enviously resent it.
There are more who accept it passively as part of the
natural order. Still others, mainly within America, are
awed by or revel in it and sometimes both. And then
there are those who, being idealistic and nostalgic for
values that seem older and truer, find it a source of anguish and dismay, fearing that power breeds arrogance
as surely as it creates responsibilities. But only very few
dispute the truth of the assertion, which is supported
by every conventional yardstick.

The North American continent is vastly endowed
and still largely underdeveloped. There is no land hunger. Its people can feed themselves on fewer and fewer
acres thanks to advances in agricultural techniques,
even if the food itself does tend to get blander and duller
to the palate. As for natural resources, water, power and
minerals, lakes and rivers, these are boundless, too, even
if waste and pollution are currently emerging as a
national nightmare.

Americans are poor on cash incomes that exceed
those of all but the richest citizens in most countries of
the world—even if one in seven of them goes to bed

hungry. Yet the Government spends millions subsidizing big farmers to hold back the planting of grains, and buys in surpluses as price-support that then cost millions more to store. Such paradoxes abound. The explanation lies in politics. There are still millions of Americans who live in hovels, yet if all the cars that wind up in a year on the nation's rubbish dumps were shipped to Africa the number of vehicles on that continent's roads would be doubled at a stroke—and loud would be the lamentation of the motor industry around the globe, including Detroit's. The waste industry is the biggest and least dispensable of all.

America's Gross National Product jumped from $700,000 million to $900,000 million between 1966 and 1969—or by rather more than the total GNP for both Britain and France together in a single year of that span. Economists differ in computing and interpreting GNP figures but it seems safe to say that Britain and Western Europe, with a population at least a quarter as big again as that of the United States, currently produce less than two-thirds as much in goods and services. Russia's GNP is less than half that of America and its population rather larger. The annual turnover of the General Motors Corporation is greater than that of Belgium. And so on....

America is rich and getting richer, all the indicators say. But Americans as individuals may not be—or not so that they themselves can sense it, which is what really matters in domestic political terms. The state of the economy is a constant worry. There are plenty of soothsayers nowadays warning of temporary setbacks and some would even argue that a recession is needed to cool inflation. But it is still heresy to talk of slumps ahead. Washington's economists are Keynesians to a man. A touch on the tax brakes here and a boost in

Federal spending there and disaster must surely be averted. Even the gloomiest forecasters—those who look to a spell of rising inflation coinciding with unemployment, soaring interest rates but falling profits all at once in the immediate future generally take a sanguine view of long-range prospects.

Moreover, America has become the keystone of the entire non-Communist world's economic structure. It might be further stated that not even the leaders of the Communist world would be happy to see the US collapse merely to vindicate their textbook theories. It would upset the symmetry of power which is essential to global order. American economic power suits most of mankind at present.

What is disturbing about this power and wealth is how quickly it has come about. Is it really secure? It seems to us today as immutable as the laws of the Medes and the Persians. It did not to our fathers, thirty-odd years ago. And there is the rub. In 1939, all the same fundamental prerequisites of prosperity existed in America: but the nation was prostrate, still far from recovered from the Great Depression that came on the heels of the Wall Street crash of 1929.

At the outbreak of the Second World War in Europe, there were still nearly 10 million Americans unemployed, or 17 per cent of the country's labour force. This was, to be sure, an improvement on the 1932 jobless peak of over 12.7 million, at which time the only nation suffering from a higher proportion of workless was Germany (a prime factor in the rise of Nazism). America's population was actually declining: births were not keeping up with deaths and for the years 1933 and 1934 there was a net exodus of migrants from the land of hope and opportunity to the Old World—a situation which only reversed itself by 1936 as refugees from the

Hitler terror began trekking West in large numbers. There were even pundits to argue consolingly at that time that America had achieved 'maturity' and that its stability would be enhanced by a contracting of horizons.

Much has been written by eminent authorities about the causes of the 1929 crash and world-wide slump that followed. We are told it could not happen again. The wild wave of speculation that had every other office boy, waiter, cab driver and housemaid caught up in a spree of stock buying on margin in the belief that the market was in a boom that could never end cannot be repeated. These little people were wiped out along with tens of thousands of the wealthier and presumably wiser because as prices tumbled they could not meet their brokers' margin calls. Today, the rules require that shares traded on the New York market must be 80 per cent covered—that is, paid for—to cushion a fall[1] But the snag remains that millions of Americans to-day are vastly over-extended in other forms of debt.

Every measure adopted in the interest of checking inflation has a loophole. The high price of borrowing becomes an accelerator rather than a brake. Revolving consumer credit arrangements have escalated with a wild proliferation of charge-cards. Capital is tight, so the banks have taken to dealing in commercial paper— a way of ballooning credit in the form of loans against security that can be quite ephemeral. In such a situation, a relatively small squeeze can force modest and even fairly substantial individual investors to sell shares at a loss simply to meet their tradesmen's bills. There is, in short, a distinct feeling of *déjà vu* about the US economy as we enter the decade of the 1970s. And this

[1] In May 1970, in an attempt to slow down a collapse in share prices, that margin requirement was cut to 65 per cent.

is certainly heightened if one re-reads some of the writings about an ebullient America that poured from the presses on both sides of the Atlantic in the mid-1920s.

In 1927, Edgar Ansell Mowrer, then a rising young foreign correspondent, later to win a Pulitzer prize for his coverage of Hitler's Germany, which got him expelled from that country, wrote a fascinating book entitled—*This American World*. His fellow expatriate, the poet T. S. Eliot, wrote an approving preface for it. Much of *This American World* could have been published, unaltered in the 1960s. It opens thus:

'The United States of America are an increasingly powerful factor in the shaping of contemporary history. For not only do they enjoy an enviable well-being but they have had the good fortune to achieve spiritual independence and the requisites of material dominion at the moment when world development had reached a point hospitable to their manners and methods. On this account that elusive, composite but vividly real something mankind is learning to call "Americanism" seems destined to spread over much of the earth.…'

Mowrer proceeded in this vein to underscore the superiority of American to European practice in business and industry. Understandably, if a trifle smugly, he ascribed this to the virtues of character developed from the rigours of life on the Western Frontier—social mobility, resourcefulness, energy and drive. He observed that Europe was fast becoming Americanized against the will of its effete intelligentsia and entrenched aristocracy. He predicted that the Germans would be quickest to adopt the then-new mass production techniques. The vacuum cleaner and the 'electric ice-box' were finding favour, along with chewing-gum, 'amongst the lower classes'. He quoted admiringly the dictum of his countryman, Henry Ford, upon seeing his first Rembrandt: 'What is the good of it? Multiply it by a million and I'll help you circulate it!'

He was not alone. Bertrand Russell, writing in the same period, if less enthusiastically, argued that the United States was sure to dominate the world. In his *Prospects of Industrial Civilization*, he said: 'America may not as yet consciously desire [to do so] but no nation with sufficient resources can long resist the attempt'. He then listed the material factors to back his statement and concluded witheringly, as his clinching argument: 'The Americans surpass even the British in the skilful use of hypocrisy by which even themselves are deceived. Against such a combination...no existing state could hope to prove victorious.'

Three decades before Jean-Jacques Servan-Schreiber, the one-time Gaullist editor of *l'Express*, published *Le Défi Americain*—a best-seller in 1968—which warned against America's irresistible imperialistic thrust into Europe, Andre Seigfried was saying much the same in *America Comes of Age*. 'Every American, whether he is called Wilson, Bryan or Rockefeller, is an evangelist who cannot let people alone,' he wrote. 'He feels the constant duty to preach at them.'

Again, like Servan-Schreiber, but 35 years ahead of him, was Paul Valéry, who pointed out how European businessmen fell all over one another in their eagerness to facilitate the American take-over of their industry. The canny French bourgeois would today rather put his money into IBM than *Machines Bull* for the excellent reason that he believes the US firm has more know-how in computers than its French rival. And so it was in the 1920s, for, to quote Valéry: 'Europe aspires visibly to being governed by an American commission. Being unable to get rid of our history, we Europeans shall be relieved of it by happy peoples who will impose their happiness upon us.' The Pursuit of Happiness—Thomas Jefferson's phrase—being enshrined in America's Declaration of Independence as an 'unalienable right', was to be inflicted on the Old World. And Europe, he concluded, with a nod to the then-current phenomenon of American prohibition, 'will be punished . . . deprived of its wines and its beer, and of other things as well.'

The Middle Western Mowrer could hardly be blamed for concluding in *This American World* that it was the destiny of the United States to emerge 'a more powerful, more humane, more educated, more democratic and more glorious Rome. . . .' With America, as with Rome, he wrote, 'business is the essence of politics and life is organized for promoting the commonwealth, the *res publica*, as the business leaders conceive it. Comfort and hygiene are the highest ideals. The Roman traveller in Greece must have been similar in the indulgent superiority of the American tourist in Europe: both peoples distrusted foreigners in spite of considerable familiarity with them. Neither had any respect for the systematic philosophy, or intellectuals. Rome anticipated the Anglo-American tendency towards successful empiricism in politics, and conquered peoples in order to civilize them. . . .

'We possess power to a degree that no previous men have dreamed of. . . . Our American task is to accept our time and within the limits of its possibilities, to express ourselves as fully and ideally as our powers permit. If we do this frankly and without hypocrisy, we shall at least secure passage through the pallid vestibule of hell and accept the future without flinching. This was the way of the pioneers who made our country.

This was the Roman way, and we should not be less than the Romans.'

Only two years after *This American World* appeared, the bottom fell right out of it. In many ways, the United States suffered more severely from the Great Depression than any other democracy, if only because its peoples' hopes had soared so high beforehand. It came as a crushing blow to self-esteem and youthful dream alike. Indeed, during the darkest days of crisis in Washington in 1932 voices were raised calling for extreme solutions.

There were Senators who spoke openly of the need for an American Mussolini, so scared they were of what they discerned as incipient red revolution. Washington was invaded by tens of thousands of jobless war veterans who threatened to march on Congress to claim 'bonus' pension money that had never been paid them. It took cavalry with drawn swords and infantry with bayonets fixed and clouds of tear gas to disperse them— an operation led by General Douglas MacArthur, who was later to win fame less controversially, with a Major Dwight Eisenhower as his aide. It was a time of soup kitchens, farm foreclosures, apple sellers on the street corners and 'Buddy, can you spare a dime?'

It is easy to forget now, more than a generation later, that the nation that elected the patrician liberal Democrat, Franklin Delano Roosevelt, as its President in 1932, was hardly reckoned a serious world power—except potentially perhaps—for the rest of the decade. The lure of the mighty dollar had faded fast in Europe when, thanks to the eccentricities of Roosevelt's favoured economic advisers in the early New Deal era, the US currency was even shakier than sterling—a difficult fact to believe today.

FDR, for all his humane virtues, was singularly vulnerable to quacks. Surely one of the weirdest in his circle was George Warren, an agronomy professor of Utica, New York, who sold him the idea that the way to cure deflation—the inverse affliction to that now threatening America's economy—was to bid up the price of gold in terms of dollars. Gold price, he insisted on the basis of his own arcane studies, was linked directly to commodity prices and the wheat price in particular. American farmers were going bankrupt in droves because they were being forced to sell their crops for less than the cost of raising them: they were being literally hounded from their land because they could not meet their mortgage payments. This could be stopped only if grain prices were pushed up: the greedy, wicked bankers could be held at bay, gnashing their teeth in frustration. How to push up the prices? Simple, said Warren. All that was required was for the US Treasury to start buying up gold in the world's bullion markets, insistently offering more than the asking price. This would devalue the dollar—and indeed it did: all the way from $20 to the fine ounce of gold to its present level of $35. But unhappily grain prices remained stubbornly low.

This kind of tinkering, which can be likened to attempting to slow down a motor car by jamming a screwdriver into the speedometer, had a shattering effect all around the world and not least amongst those holding dollars in the otherwise reasonable belief that America was the land of promise. In the very long run, of course, their faith was justified—just as was that of anyone who could have afforded to ride out the Wall Street crash and hang on to blue chip shares until they eventually recovered and burgeoned anew. But such antics do explain why international bankers of his generation still shudder at the recollection of FDR's 'funny money' men.

America in the 1930s similarly enjoyed scant reputation as a military power. With two oceans to defend, the US Navy had been allowed to run down far beyond the perilous 5:5:3 ratio set under the Washington Agreement of 1922 for capital ship tonnage between America, Britain and Japan. Indeed, only a few months before the Japanese sneak attack on Pearl Harbour on December 9th, 1941, Admiral James Richardson, then commander of the US Pacific Fleet in Hawaii, submitted his resignation rather than carry out a Presidential order to move a squadron to Manila in the Philippines. He told Roosevelt, as his C-in-C, that he assumed he had in mind that the ships should be ready to go into action and, if this were so, he could not in good conscience concur since it was his judgement that they needed a complete refit on the West Coast before they could be deemed battle worthy. His resignation was accepted— but he was rapidly vindicated by the success of the Japanese attack.

The US Army, also, had scant prestige, either at home or abroad. It is true the Marine Corps had a certain dubious distinction earned in sundry Caribbean police actions, but the US Air Force, as such, did not even exist, except as a branch of the Army and Navy respectively. There was no military service tradition in America to speak of in those days: it was not the 'done thing' for the sons of the well-to-do to serve 'with the Regiment'. The Forces were kept starved of funds and were resented by solid, taxpaying businessmen as a haven for second-raters who could not make the grade in the real world, as they saw it. There is certainly no evidence that Hitler, for one, was impressed by the notion that American power would ultimately crush him.

It is conventional wisdom nowadays to hold that

Roosevelt had always meant to get America into the Second World War. It is easy to find diehard isolationist Republicans who insist to this day that the Japanese attack on Pearl Harbour was deliberately provoked in order to justify his declaration against the Axis. Legends about the dead are not easily refuted. One can only say that it did not seem very probable at the time.

We are more often told now that the late Joseph Kennedy, the American ambassador to Britain over the Munich period and up to the London blitz, fell out with FDR over policy. An ardent 'America firster', he was convinced that the British would collapse, nothing could stop Hitler and that therefore the US should remain firmly neutral. If his President disagreed with him, one must observe that he was careful not to make it clear before he was safely re-elected for his third term in the White House in 1940. He went out of his way to praise his 'beloved' ambassador when drumming up the Irish vote in Kennedy's native Boston. American public opinion was decidedly not in favour of direct involvement in the war then and nobody knew it better than FDR.

I myself recall lesser Americans being most emphatically neutral, although on the whole kindly disposed towards Britain and impressed, if a trifle grudgingly at first, by British fortitude in the face of German bombing. But there were great doubts as to whether the British could hold out, even if it were later to become the 'in' thing to send off 'Bundles for Britain'.

In Cairo in 1941, when I was a stringer for the United Press, I took a visiting vice-president of the American agency named Virgil Pinkney to meet an Egyptian editor whom he wished to sign up with a UP contract. He made his sales pitch America's neutrality. He told the Egyptian: 'We can offer you an impartial, *neutral* news service that will give you objective reports, without fear or favour—unlike Reuters, which is controlled by the British Government.' He was a trifle taken aback when the editor replied gently: 'Very interesting, my dear sir. But I feel you should know that mine is not a neutral newspaper!' A week later the Japanese attack came. This time Pinkney fared better: he made his sale to *Al Moussawa* on the strength of that.

It is difficult at this distance to appreciate it fully, but the records show that America was headed into a severe slump in 1938—a relapse from the brief upturn in 1936 —and was only rescued in the nick of time by the collective folly of the Europeans in getting into a second war in a generation. Contrary to popular folklore, it was not instantly galvanized into action, hammering out the sinews of war. When Paul Reynaud of France made his piteous plea in the name of Lafayette for Roosevelt to rush a 'cloud of aeroplanes' to save his country from the onrushing German hordes in 1940, the American leader could not respond: there was no such cloud available. The US was to get into high gear later, to be sure, but it took time, for which Britain paid dearly although it is not generally considered polite these days to labour that point.

Eliot Janeway, the splendidly no-nonsense New York economic analyst, pointed out in *The Economics of Crisis*: 'America's economic mobilization to hold the line first for England and then for Russia boomed the economy. But Hitler could have brought both Russia and England to their knees, as he did Western Europe, and America still would not have gone to war. It took the monumental irrationality of Pearl Harbour to free America to bring the power of her economy to bear', unhampered by Rooseveltian 'planning'. Janeway says that America only really became the arsenal of

democracy once FDR was compelled by events to concentrate on war leadership and stop interfering with
industry, letting the production managers get on with
the job the way they knew best.

It was, needless to say, highly profitable for those
concerned. Whether or not Roosevelt led his people into
war for this or for loftier motives is beside the point.
But the Four Freedoms he had Winston Churchill en-
dorse in the Atlantic Charter in 1941, in return for
lend-lease after Britain's last reserves had been drained
dry buying essential supplies on the previous cash-and-
carry basis, certainly provided a pious gloss to an otherwise hard-headed policy of protecting a not inconsiderable US investment in the survival of democracy. One
somehow doubts that Britain's bulldog wartime Prime
Minister was vastly impressed by pledges to banish
Hunger and Want from this earth; to guarantee Freedom of Speech and Religion. The right of all people to
self-determination sounded fine, too. But what was
infinitely more significant and meaningful was the
super-secret decision at that time to go ahead and un-
cork the nuclear genii.

It was this, the development of the atomic bomb,
which transformed everything. By the time the shoot-
ing was over, there could be no doubt whatsoever: a
super-power was born. Even without The Bomb, none
could challenge it: with it, who would? Yet even then,
odd though it is to recollect it now, many if not most
Americans were blissfully unaware that their status in
the world had been totally revolutionized.

The searing experience of the Depression had left its
mark. The US was now the one and only Power, but
was not eager to accept it. Americans by and large
wanted nothing more than to return as rapidly as
possible to peacetime living, not to become involved in

overseas complications. The prevailing attitude of America's opinion-makers in the aftermath of the war tended towards censoriousness—towards the British not least.

The British had long been imperialist tyrants, had they not? It was time they were humbled. It was a popular American view that snobbish, class-conscious rulers had displayed gutlessness against Hitler at Munich. They had distrusted the Russians earlier and now, all of a sudden, they were trying to make out that Uncle Joe Stalin, that fine, friendly fellow puffing away at his pipe, was a menace. They were trying to set the GI up against G-Ivan, who was plainly a doughty, if uncouth ally. There was reason to suspect that this was merely part of a cunning plot to enlist America's help in the re-establishment of the British Empire. In Palestine, the British were forcibly denying unlimited entry to the survivors of Hitler's monstrous 'final solution' on the plainly specious plea, as Americans saw it, that the Arabs objected. This seemed so clearly false that the screenwriter, Ben Hecht, was warmly applauded when he proclaimed that he 'sang a little song' in his heart every time another British soldier was shot dead. Of course, America was not exactly opening wide her gates to Europe's Jewish refugees, but what of it? They were holding Irgun Zvei Leumi fund drives in Madison Square Garden instead.

Against this presumption of Britain's imperialistic nature, it struck Americans as paradoxical that its people should have elected a socialist Government in 1945. But this was interpreted as a sign of decadence in another context—proof of which was their readiness to go on living on handouts from ever-generous Uncle Sam.

The intellectual climate of America at that time, of

course, had been formed by the apparent collapse of capitalism in the preceding decade. Parlour pinks abounded. Relatively few Americans had had the opportunity to discover before the mushroom clouds rose over Hiroshima and Nagasaki that our erstwhile Communist comrades-in-arms were not exactly the 'freedom-loving friends' wartime propaganda had made them out to be. The Cold War was yet to come—or rather it had begun without most people realizing it.

The understandable American instinct was, in any case, one commended by none other than George Washington in his farewell address: namely, to eschew foreign entanglements. So it was entirely logical, although most upsetting to the rest of us, that President Truman was scarcely to let the ink dry on the Japanese surrender document before he cancelled lend-lease. History seemed to be repeating itself with a vengeance. Hardly anyone would have then predicted that a generation later there would still be about a million US servicemen overseas. It seemed clear that America would revert to that spirit of isolationism which led to the rejection of President Wilson's efforts in 1920 to join the new-found League of Nations. True, America had been trapped into the latest substitute, the United Nations, but it still remained to be seen how much that was actually to mean—beyond providing a useful pulpit from which to preach at one's former allies about liberating their colonial subjects from imperialist exploitation.

American ambivalence towards Britain and also towards Communism in those days showed up in all sorts of odd ways. Had Roosevelt lived, can one really be sure he would have fully awoken to the realities ahead after the Yalta Conference? My own hunch is that he, and even more especially those close to him, were of a mind to make a deal with the Kremlin to cut those tiresome old reactionaries in Europe down to size. There is ample evidence he wanted to force the French out of Indochina and North Africa, the Dutch out of Indonesia and the British out of India and her other colonies. He would have made a present of Hong Kong to Generalissimo Chiang Kai Shek. The Chinese Nationalists were, in fact, awarded North Vietnam as a post-war Occupation zone—with the object of edging the French out of their colony. Had Roosevelt had his way, as things worked out later, it would have turned the entire Eurasian land mass from the English Channel to the Bering Straits over to Communist rule.

In December 1944 in Greece, when Churchill ordered British paratroops to intervene to prevent the Communist-led ELAS guerillas from seizing Athens by force in a well-planned coup, the American Press was almost unanimously critical, not to say outright hostile. The picture was conjured up of peace-loving, anti-fascist liberals being savagely crushed in order that a detested monarch, King George II of the Hellenes, should be imposed on them to preserve British imperial interests in the Mediterranean. What if there were Communists amongst them or even dominating them? Were they not stout allies of ours in the struggle against Hitler? The fact that the majority of Greeks thought otherwise was readily overlooked.

I was personally caught in the middle of this situation because I happened to be a war correspondent for the Associated Press of America at the time. A well-known colleague representing the *Chicago Daily News* wrote a furious despatch denouncing the AP for employing a 'youthful Englishman' on such a delicate assignment. In his eyes, I was obviously biased, whereas any American would be better fitted to see things his way. There were, happily, only a handful of US air-force ground personnel to clutter the scene, yet I fear they made a great nuisance of themselves with their insistent neutrality. Memorably irritating at the time was the over-zealous attaché at the US Embassy, which happened to form a salient in the frontline of the street fighting at one point, who objected to British soldiers drawing water from Ambassador Lincoln McVeagh's garden on the grounds that it would compromise his position *vis-à-vis* the insurgents. There was also a reporter from a New York paper on hand, who insisted on his right to cross the lines at will to carry on his journalistic functions. Our Intelligence had solid grounds for suspecting that he was a spy. It later transpired that he was, indeed, a fullblown Communist Party member and in due course, some years later, he defected to Rumania.

Controversy was not confined to the Press. Churchill was strongly criticized in Washington by the ailing Roosevelt's Secretary of State, Edward Stettinius. As Churchill noted rather mildly later, Stettinius issued 'a markedly critical pronouncement' concerning the British intervention at precisely the moment when it was best calculated to encourage ELAS to further efforts in the belief that the uprising enjoyed US backing. Had it succeeded, Athens and all Greece would surely have been swallowed up by the Communists. As an eyewitness to the red terror in the Peleponnese and Attica in areas under ELAS control during the immediate post-liberation period, I was under no illusions as to what that would have meant. The British Prime Minister was absolutely right.

Britain was not alone in suffering from the anticolonialist fervour that characterized FDR's Administration. General de Gaulle had scant reason to love the Americans who had persistently tried to downgrade him in favour of General Giraud as the recognized French liberation leader. In 1945, de Gaulle wanted to send a small mission to Hanoi to re-establish the French presence in North Vietnam—or Indochina, as it then was. This was deliberately blocked for several weeks on direct orders from Washington. Eventually de Gaulle's special envoy, a skilful underground veteran, Jean Sainteny, contrived to bluff the US authorities in Chungking. He reached Hanoi and established relations with the Vietnamese leader, Ho Chi Minh. It is ironical to reflect that Ho was enjoying US support at that time as a patriot leader. The wheel was to turn a complete circle: the American OSS liaison officer (OSS being the forerunner of the Central Intelligence Agency) assigned to Ho was Major Joseph Patti, who was later to serve on President Johnson's White House staff. And Jean Sainteny was sent by de Gaulle 22 years later to Hanoi on another mission—this time to try and work out with Ho some compromise peace solution in Vietnam that the US could accept. He failed.

American views on the global scene in the immediate aftermath of World War II were surely overdue to undergo an about-face, but as late as 1946, when Sir Winston made his famous speech at Fulton, Missouri, warning that an 'Iron Curtain has descended across Europe' from Stettin to Trieste there were cries of dismay from many prominent Washington pundits—and a few from Britain, too. It was not yet fashionable to observe such painful truths. But as the war leader was later able to write: 'It is odd looking back on these events to see how completely the policy for which I and my colleagues had fought so stubbornly has been justified by events.'

He added: 'I little thought at the end of 1944 that the State Department, supported by overwhelming American opinion, would in little more than two years not only adopt and carry on the course we had opened, but would make vehement and costly exertions, even of a military character, to bring it to fruition.'

4

How the US Assumed the Mantle

It must be rarely that it happens that one can put one's finger on the precise moment when the tide of history turned. But in this case one can. The moment when, as the participants themselves saw it, America took over the torch, was at 4.00 p.m. on a cold, damp February afternoon in Washington: February 21, 1947. In London, in the grip of the bitterest winter in memory, made all the worse by coal shortages, power cuts and the accumulated weariness of war recently ended, it was already night.

The issue was Greece and Turkey, both of whom had been promised British support and who were facing serious Russian pressure. In Greece the Communists had recovered, in part owing to the excesses of the extreme Right following the Communist failure to seize power in 1945. There had been a reaction in favour of the Communists, and their guerilla forces were in the ascendancy once more. In Turkey, Moscow was laying claim on the eastern provinces of Kars and Ardahan. But Britain was no longer in a position, economically, to sustain the effort of meeting either country's requirements for arms and equipment beyond March 13. Greece alone would have to have £40 million in relief supplies to survive the year, and to reorganize her military forces would cost as much again. The Chancellor of the Exchequer, Hugh Dalton, had told Ernest Bevin,

74

the Foreign Secretary, that it was simply not on. And that was that.

Lord Inverchapel, the British Ambassador in Washington, was duly instructed to inform General George Marshall, the Secretary of State. But Marshall had already left his office for the weekend. The matter seemed so pressing that H. M. Sichel, a first secretary, was sent round at once to deliver advance copies of the relevant notes—one on Greece and the other, briefer, on Turkey—to Loy Henderson, who was then in charge of the Office of Near Eastern Affairs. Marshall's Undersecretary was Dean Acheson. As fate would have it, this singularly tough-minded Washington company lawyer, who was to become one of the principal architects of the post-war world, was still at his desk.

Years later Henderson recalled it as one of the most dramatic moments of his career. 'As soon as we read the notes,' he told me, 'we realized at once what it meant. We took it to Mr. Acheson. And he set us right away to preparing the necessary staff papers for what was to emerge as the Truman Doctrine. The immediate thing was clear: the gap must be plugged. It would call for new legislation. An immense amount of groundwork would have to be laid to ensure Congressional support. Just as soon as we read those notes, I can tell you, we all knew that Great Britain had, there and then, handed the job of world leadership to the United States.'

What had started out as a simple plea that America should pick up the bill for support costs for Greece and Turkey was swiftly expanded in Acheson's fertile mind into a far broader conception. Bevin's heart-cry, after all, had come on the heels of British withdrawals that had already begun in Burma and were soon to follow in India. As Acheson was later to remark, causing considerable ire in Fleet Street, 'Britain has lost an Empire but has yet to find a role!' Acheson to this day affects the style and appearance of the English patrician of a bygone age—Hollywood would have no trouble casting him in the kind of role the late C. Aubrey Smith used to play: the harrumphing retired general in *The Four Feathers*, for example. It is somehow fitting that such a figure should have so eagerly seized on the role abandoned by Britain.

During the war, Acheson had been co-opted into Government service and had occupied himself with organizing America's economic blockade of Germany. He did not come into his own until the Truman era. Harry Truman was later to describe him as the greatest Secretary since John Quincy Adams—an equally hard-nosed patrician in his day. Credit has since been given to men like George Kennan, the career foreign service officer whose experience in Russia led him to advocate in a famous *Foreign Affairs* article, published under the pseudonym 'X', the so-called Policy of Containment, for turning American policy around. In fact, Kennan had reservations about trying to save Turkey and was even doubtful about Greece. In Henderson's view it was Acheson who 'fought it through. Truman saw what we were driving at right away. But selling it to Congress was something else.'

Britain had already had her first big American loan. The American electorate would not take kindly to the idea of stumping up for her Mediterranean satellites, as they were sure to be regarded. It would savour of pulling her chestnuts out of the fire. Moreover, sympathies regarding the British were very mixed at the time: the Zionists were portraying them as oppressors of the Jews. Anti-colonialism was very much in vogue. And in Greece itself, Britain was pictured as being in league with 'monarcho-fascists' against 'freedom-loving democrats'

—the Communist guerillas having cannily adopted the title 'Democratic Army' to lend colour to this notion.

Acheson used that weekend well. He got his staff to split up into working parties to liaise with the Pentagon, to dredge up facts, figures and background notes. In short, he had instant studies assembled on every conceivable subject from Russia's historical grand strategy in relation to the Dardanelles, the vulnerability of the West's Middle East oil reserves, down to such nuts-and-bolts items as the availability of American military hardware and advisers that could be swiftly despatched to the danger area. As a result of this remarkable *tour de force*, General Marshall was fully primed even before Inverchapel paid his formal call at the State Department the following Monday to present the Bevin notes to Truman's Secretary of State.

But the job did not end there. Next task was to sell the blueprint to Congress and the nation. Here again Acheson made the running. Marshall very nearly fumbled it when the Congressional leaders of both parties were summoned to the White House on February 27 to be briefed on the crisis that, up to that moment, had barely surfaced in public.

'Although he thoroughly understood the strategic significance of Greece and Turkey,' said James Jones, one of Acheson's team, a generation later, 'Marshall failed to put it across. He conveyed the impression that aid should be extended to Greece on grounds of loyalty and humanitarianism, and to Turkey to strengthen Britain's position in the Middle East. This did not go down well with Congressmen whose major preoccupation was reducing aid abroad and taxes at home. Their initial reaction was rather trivial and adverse. They wanted to know how much it was going to cost and what we were letting ourselves in for.'

Seeing the discussion slithering from Marshall's grasp, Acheson butted in with an aside: 'Is this a private fight or can anyone join in?' Marshall, as an old soldier, might have resented such an intrusion from anyone else: instead he asked Truman to let his subordinate take over, which he proceeded to do with considerable passion and effect. He ripped into the suggestion that aid to Greece and Turkey was merely a way of bailing out the British. He brushed aside as irrelevant the humanitarian plea. He pointed out that if Russia, directly or through subversion, was to gain control of two-thirds of the world's surface there could be no security for the United States and freedom everywhere would have a poor chance of survival.

A hush fell on the cabinet room when he finished. It was broken at last by the venerable Senator Arthur Vandenburg, the Republican leader and, in his day, an isolationist. He had been impressed and shaken and said so. He urged Truman to speak directly to Congress and the nation and promised him bipartisan backing. On March 12, this was duly done.

In asking for the first $400 million for aid to the two Mediterraneon states, the key passage in the Truman Doctrine then enunciated laid it down as the policy of the United States 'to support free peoples who are resisting attempted subjugation by armed minorities or outside pressures' and 'to assist them to work out their destinies in their own way.' Failure to do so, he went on, would be disastrous not only for Greece and Turkey but for free institutions the world over. 'Great responsibilities have been placed upon us by the swift movement of events,' Truman concluded, 'but I am confident the Congress will face up to them squarely.'

Thus was the die cast. But for Acheson's ginger group it was only the start. No time was wasted in expanding on the basic Truman Doctrine. Reports of a deepening economic crisis and impending political unrest resulting from it began to pour back from the rest of Western Europe. An even bigger rescue operation was required and the American people were going to have to be persuaded about that, too. They had not yet fully accepted the looming intervention in Greece: opposition to the idea of becoming involved there, and to this general cause that was to become known as 'containing Communism', was still strong. The American press had still not got the message.

Nowadays it might be supposed that the United States was eager to assume the grandeur of world leadership 'with its burdens and its glory'—to quote James Jones again. Not a bit of it. A substantial segment of public opinion was firmly against it. Indeed, most reports from American foreign correspondents out of Greece at that time were heavily critical of the Tsaldaris Government in power in Athens and tending to favour the guerillas as, at worst, misled liberals who could readily be coaxed into abandoning their armed struggle if a coalition government was installed.

This was the view, for example, of the *New York Times'* Homer Bigart, who interviewed the rebel chieftain, Marcos Vefiades, in his mountain HQ. To achieve this Bigart had made an adventurous crossing from Yugoslavia into Greece. That Bigart's own exploit tended to prove that the Yugoslavs were helping the so-called Democratic Army seemed almost beside the point. It was Bigart and others of his persuasion who were the pace-setters at that time.

When George Polk, the correspondent for the Columbia Broadcasting System, tried to emulate him by crossing into rebel territory from inside Greece, he had less luck. I had succeeded in doing this; but I had taken care to get myself 'captured' by the guerillas in circumstances that would seem to them like a reasonably honest error by getting 'lost' in the mountains in a snowstorm. Polk was more ambitious. Having widely advertised his intentions, he proceeded to contact Communist agents in Salonika and, in the process, plainly acquired too much compromising information for his own health. He allowed himself to be taken blindfold on to a sailing boat, in the belief that he would be transported in it to a rendezvous with Marcos. Since he carried on his person identification that attested to his status as a reserve officer in the US Marines—he had, indeed, served heroically as a pilot in the Pacific during the war—he was almost certainly suspected of being an American spy. The Truman Doctrine had, after all, just been enunciated at the time.

Poor Polk was shot dead and dumped in the sea. A week or so later his body was found. Immediately there was a hue and cry. It was widely asserted that he had fallen victim to a right-wing terrorist, if not to deliberate police action. In the mood of the times, it seemed to many Americans logical that the Tsaldaris Government would have wanted to get rid of a critical young American broadcaster. He was an idealist and had denounced the Athens regime loud and long for its corruption and ineptitude—in a way that was to become fashionable in Saigon much later. CBS commissioned none other than General 'Wild Bill' Donovan, wartime head of the Office of Strategic Services, the forerunner of the CIA, to fly out to Greece to investigate. Further to stimulate the political drama of the affair, it happened that Polk was the lineal descendant of the American President of that name. He had a formidable mother, a gentlewoman of the Daughters of the American Revolution breed, who also took a hand in chivvying the Greek authorities into resolving the mystery of her son's death. Eventually, a left-wing Greek journalist was charged with being an accessory to the murder, having acted as a contact, but the killers were never found.

George was a good-hearted, sincere young liberal and would have probably had a hard time had he lived on into the red-baiting heydey of Senator Joe McCarthy's anti-communist campaign. His memory is honoured yet—and properly so. There is an annual George Polk Award made by New York's Overseas Press Club to distinguished journalists in the field. He was, I believe, the first casualty of a new era—of an American Empire of which he would not have approved.

Meanwhile, back in Washington, Acheson and his men were pressing on. They were not to be distracted by such irrelevancies as the Polk affair or the doubts such incidents created or the persistent criticism by liberals and isolationists alike of the Athenians America was rescuing.

Acheson was later to entitle his memoirs: *Present at the Creation.* The phrase, he claims, originated from a remark by King Alphonso X of Spain who observed that had he been, he would have surely provided some useful hints on the better ordering of the universe. Its choice by Acheson for his book is itself revealing. He is a splendidly vain man but he has something to be vain about: it was undoubtedly due to his dynamism that the Marshall Plan was hatched.

The problem as he saw it was no longer that of determining whether United States aid was necessary to Europe's recovery. In the hard light of *real politik*, it was vital to America that the ruined Old World should be helped to recover its economic health and well-being. The survival of friendly governments and institutions depended on it. Had they collapsed west of the Iron

Curtain that Churchill had already alluded to, there was little doubt that revolutionaries hostile to all the United States stood for would soon seize power in one country after another. In time the genius of Europe would revive. But once rebuilt, its industrial capacity and resources would be dominated from Moscow. Not all of the scientists and technicians on the continent would 'choose freedom', swim the Channel or (if Britain should also succumb) make their escape across the Atlantic.

It was not a happy prospect. To prevent it materializing was, therefore, an act of enlightened self-interest rather than altruism. Yet it marked a clean break with the past. Acheson and his close allies, members all of a new breed of foreign service professionals, quite different from the do-gooder New Dealers of the 1930s, saw that it would be necessary to launch the project with peculiar skill.

The key was to get the Europeans to ask for United States assistance for a vast, co-operative scheme for mutual economic self-help, not simply to put them on an American dole. Stress was to be given to the notion of broad economic recovery rather than of buttressing America's military defences, since the latter as a prime objective would have been quickly resented. It was during this formative phase that Senator William Fulbright introduced a Congressional resolution favouring the setting up of a United States of Europe. In theory, at least, Acheson's men agreed, this could eventually come about if the beneficiaries of the plan could only be coaxed into it.

The reasons for this crabwise approach were both foreign and domestic: European pride would be affronted at the idea of begging for hand-outs, and the American puritan ethic runs sharply counter to the idea of passing any out. Acheson, therefore, took it on himself to educate public opinion a trifle more before having his chief make his move. He did this on May 8 with a major speech to a group of Mississippi delta farmers, who may well have been puzzled at the national attention they were accorded. The Deputy Secretary saw to it in advance that his utterances were well covered by the Press. The main burden of his message was that foreign aid is good business, not charity. When it was established that this thought could be uttered in a highly conservative setting without setting off any secondary explosions, General Marshall was primed to deliver his Harvard address of June 5.

The Marshall speech sketched out Europe's situation and offered America's 'full co-operation' to any Government willing to assist in a joint programme for recovery. But the initiative had to come from Europe. This was the key. The risk was that the Europeans would fail to read the signal flashed them—and they very nearly did.

Washington legend has it that Acheson calculated shrewdly that the British Embassy would probably miss their cue. He accordingly took the undiplomatic precaution of inviting three leading London newspaper reporters, including Malcolm Muggeridge of the *Daily Telegraph*, to lunch with him privately the day before it was delivered. He advised them of its importance and urged them to treat it so and transmit the text very fully to their offices. They duly complied—and it was a good thing they did, for an economy-minded Embassy official, thinking to save dollars, failed to transmit the text by cable to Downing Street. Instead it reached Ernest Bevin, page by page, as it came across the Fleet Street teleprinters and was rushed by messenger to the Foreign Office.

When the great Labour Foreign Secretary was asked

by his timid staff if they should not seek clarification from Sir John Balfour, the *chargé d'affaires* in Washington, to make sure that Marshall meant what he seemed to be saying, he simply snorted: 'No! I don't want to take any chances. I want to go on the assumption it was fully meant.' And, as he later recalled with relish: 'I seized the offer with both 'ands.'

The sequel is self-evident. The Marshall Plan took shape. It achieved the desired miracle. Europe recovered. And, from an American viewpoint, it has all paid off handsomely. It is intriguing to observe now that whereas Truman was given a hard time by Congressional cheese-parers over a $40,000 million all-in budget in 1948, twenty years later that figure would only cover roughly half the Pentagon's appropriation for defence. During the same period the Federal Government's revenues have multiplied fivefold and the nation's GNP quadrupled.[1]

The Marshall Plan established America firmly as paramount nation; and the psychological foundations for this feat had been laid in barely three months. It could never have happened had not some determined backroom boys been ready with clinching arguments to overwhelm objections. The nation's elected political leaders—including Truman himself, who had inherited the Presidency on Roosevelt's death in harness—were putty in the hands of appointed advisers.[2]

Truman's Democrats had suffered a severe reverse in the 1946 Congressional elections, losing control of both

[1] It can be argued, however—as Servan-Schreiber did in 1968—that the process may have gone altogether too far if by 1980 the third greatest economic power concentration in the world after the United States and Russia proves not to be Europe but US investment in Europe.

[2] The power of Washington's brahmins, of whom Acheson is one of the most double-dyed, was—and is—at once a source of strength and a weakness. It permits great talents to be applied to major problems in government. In an increasingly complex world

houses to the Republicans. This did not, however, inhibit the development of an activist foreign policy. Acheson, who was soon to succeed Marshall as Secretary of State, won his President's especial favour at least in part because his manners were courtly. When Truman returned to Washington by train after that electoral *débâcle*, the only member of his official team to turn up at the station to greet him, impeccable in black homburg and velvet collared greatcoat, was Acheson. He naturally never forgot it. Of such whimsical things the direction of high policy is compounded.

Had it not been for Acheson's guidance of Truman, the Russians would surely have been in the Mediterranean in Stalin's lifetime. It seemed certain at the time that after Greece and Turkey, Italy and even France would have fallen like ninepins. The French and Italian Communist Parties were enormously strong. We had not seen heresy develop within the Marxist-Leninist faith—Yugoslavia's Marshal Tito was not ejected by the Stalinists until 1949, after all. So the new American policy was bold and imaginative even if it was (quite reasonably) fundamentally self-interested.

It was to a large degree Acheson's doing that the US assumed the mantle. The snag about him, however, is that he is very far from being a typical American of today. He is a Whig aristocrat and Maryland squire, a scholar and a gentleman to his fingertips, but an anachronism. America found itself leader of the Western World in 1948—by a combination of accident and deliberate design. Was it equipped for the role? Is it now? Has Acheson been succeeded by men of the stamina his vision called for? It seems not.

this may be an advantage. But it also can result in policies being embarked upon that the nation at large will repudiate in due course through the ballot box.

5

A Manufactured Nationhood

Visiting the University of Alabama a few years ago—it was at the time when the State's then Governor, George Wallace, was preparing to 'stand in the schoolhouse door' to bar the entry of that college's first two black undergraduates—my attention was caught by a notice on the board in the Students' Union. It advised freshmen of what appeared to be a new regulation. It read: 'As from this semester it will be a tradition that...' As I recall the rest had to do with first-year scholars not being permitted to walk down a certain path across the campus' main lawn and that they must wear a particular headgear.

It is unfair to make fun of this kind of thing but not to observe in it evidence that very many Americans do suffer from the absence of a Past. Ideally, America, free of ancient feuds and phobias, should be the crucible from which the first truly Universal Man will emerge. Unfortunately this has not happened. Instead a fabricated nationalism has emerged. In the Old World, nationality is instinctively a part of one. The American is subtly different: to preserve his sense of nationality, he must constantly remind himself of it. He can lose his citizenship by the mere act of voting in another country's elections or joining its armed forces. A Briton or a Frenchman cannot lose his nationality, no matter how disgracefully he behaves—he can only lose certain rights. The American's nationalism shares all the defects of chauvinism but few of the cohesive natural attributes of older societies.

An element of insecurity has long been characteristic of the American psyche. Alexis de Tocqueville remarked in 1831 that the Americans he met on his travels were 'impatient of the smallest censure, insatiable of praise', being in need of constant reassurance about the superiority of his condition if only because it was 'very fluctuating (and) almost always recently acquired'. The young French nobleman, indeed, found it 'remarkable that two nations [Britain and America] so recently sprung from the same stock should be so opposite to one another in their manner of feeling and conversing.' And maybe not too much has changed since his day.

To Americans, the nation exists almost as a religion. The Stars and Stripes has an especial sanctity in their eyes. The casual way the British nowadays have of using Union Jacks for shopping bags or bikini bottoms would be utterly intolerable to millions of solid Middle Americans. There was a huge outcry a few years ago when some enterprising merchant bought up quantities of superseded flags—the old 48-star version being outdated by the accession of Hawaii and Alaska as States of the Union—and shipped them off to Africa where they were cut up into colourful garments to cover the nakedness of primitive bushmen. The disclosure that this outrage had been made possible under the US Foreign Aid programme added injury to insult.

Every American schoolchild begins his classroom day incanting the pledge of allegiance, facing the flag. This, one is told, is necessary to inculcate a sense of national unity and high purpose. It is seen as peculiarly desirable and even necessary to bring together people drawn from the four corners of the earth. By the same token, the Supreme Court has ruled that prayers may not be read in public schools because it would counter the doctrine of separation of Church and State. Doubtless in the era of unrestricted immigration before the First World War, it helped stir the great melting pot. And it surely is a fact that to this day no one exceeds in patriotic fervour those whom snobbish New Englanders are wont to term 'hyphenated Americans'—usually referred to in the jargon of machine politics at election time as 'the ethnic vote'—and the proudest are often those with unpronounceable names composed entirely of consonants.

To them, of course, the United States was truly a land of golden opportunity compared with the oppression, whether economic or political or both, they had fled. Despite the trials and disillusionments, particularly of the 1930s, it remains so with their descendants. It is only amongst the rising generation of the 1960s, and now the 1970s, that rejection of that proposition is taking place—and then only within an articulate minority.

The founders of the Republic, however, were plantation owners, gentlemen farmers and professional men, more of them scholars than merchants, who took their time about drafting the American Constitution. The framers of that remarkable document can hardly have foreseen the expansion of the country from 13 to 50 States or from 4 million to over 200 million people in two centuries. The main purpose they achieved by means of a series of compromises was the prevention of strong, centralized government. As the immediate descendants of colonists, who had for the most part rebelled quite reluctantly against the motherland, they were idealists. One, for example, urged that the Federal standing army should never exceed 3,000 men in number and wanted this specifically stipulated in the Constitution. They felt that no individual should ever have too much say over his fellows and that sovereignty should always reside as far as possible in the member states. The arrangement was, perhaps, perfect for the ordering of a gentlemen's club: hardly for the government of a major world power. But fate—and the arrival on an immense scale of new blood from sources vividly different from the original stock—ordained that the latter would come into being.

The Founding Fathers were an aristocracy of intellect for their times. But the nation they created grew great because the diligent pursuit of gain, comforts and all the more mundane but practical considerations of life interested the broad masses far more. To harp on the democratic ideals espoused by the Founders has been useful cement to hold the American nation together. Respect for the rule of law and the liberty of the subject are fine slogans for the vaunted American Way of Life—yet they can have all that in tidy little confederations like Switzerland which aspire to no international leadership role. To become a dominant world power calls for something more: the elaboration of myths and motivations that can be enshrined as imperatives.

The influence of the 'new' Americans and the relative decline of the original white Anglo-Saxon protestants— the WASPs—fundamentally altered the nation's development. The non-WASP aspires to the external attributes of the WASP, to be sure, but the effort of attaining them has often been enough of an adventure to induce a narrow caution. The ruling-class WASP has tended to absorb the more aggressive strains from the new blood—but in doing so has produced a new amalgam. The successful migrant has undergone metamorphosis into pseudo-WASP: the less successful has remained an 'ethnic'. It is not surprising that the 'ethnics' should tend to be strongly isolationist. In the New World, their patriotism has a strain of desperation.

On the domestic scene it is the 'ethnics', who are still predominantly working class—'blue-collar' being the preferred Americanism—and are subtly discriminated against in all sorts of ways. It is they who most bitterly resent the pace and thrust of the Civil Rights movement. They have a deep-seated fear of the still far from emancipated black minority. They feel the black is being coddled by the affluent at their expense. They are more afraid, more resentful, than the backward Southern white, who has a deeper confidence in his national historical identity.

That constituent of the American dream which claims a classless social mobility scarcely survives today and by failing it has added a new flaw to the cohesion of American nationhood. It used to be said that Americans do not hate the rich because they aspire to be rich. It was regarded as the essence of Americanism—the key to its ebullient optimism. But of late much has happened to destroy the idea. As the world has grown more complicated to live in and with the 'knowledge explosion' widening the gulf between the trained and untrained, skilled and unskilled, new barriers have arrived to impede that cherished mobility. A college degree is now regarded as essential to an American's advancement. A chasm has thus opened up between the university graduate and the man who got no further than high school.

A certain amount of hypocrisy is no doubt a necessary ingredient in the process of nation-building. Common ground must be found upon which to construct a national heritage that all can share even if this requires a bending of the strict, unvarnished truth upon occasion. George Washington never told a lie—but he must be one of the very few revolutionaries on record to keep detailed expense accounts and the pages of them on public view in the museum at his old home, Mount Vernon, indicate he was not above padding them.

Americans generally regard themselves as anti-colonialist. This is what they learnt in school. The Founding Fathers threw off the British yoke. They refused to pay taxes on tea and dumped it in Boston Harbour. No taxation without representation, they said. But worse than that, the 'history of the present King of Great Britain is a history of repeated injuries and usurpations, all having in direct object the establishment of an absolute Tyranny' which had 'already begun with circumstances of cruelty and perfidy scarcely paralleled in the most barbarous ages', to quote the Declaration of Independence of 1776. The mad Hanoverian, George III, shipped in hateful Hessian mercenaries to crush the high-minded colonists who, being in the right, inevitably won. This is the national folklore.

The original document, enshrined in a massive, brass-bound, bulletproof case, sealed in helium gas and illumined by pale amber light to preserve it from exposure, is the centrepiece for the tomblike National Archives building in Washington. It is an object of pilgrimage. The anti-colonialist revolutionary element in the national ideal has acquired a momentum of its own but never had much substance.

Another major American tradition which has had its impact on the national culture and has also lost its relevance is the Frontier. It is not a tradition to be scoffed at. It must certainly have taken great courage and endurance to have set forth in small and vulnerable groups across the mountains and the plainlands and the deserts, ever widening the horizon. But now there is a Frontier no more, and with it has gone another facet of the corporate image in which a nation must be secure if it is to lead with confidence. Another cherished myth holds that America is the Land of the Free, where anyone can aspire to the Presidency. Log-cabin-to-the-White House is part of the dream. Yet the truth is that today it costs several hundred million dollars to put a party's nominee into the White House. Politics is not for little people any more. Then it was perhaps once true that opportunity beckoned the enterprising individualist. Now the truth is that the vast majority of Americans work for giant corporations. The man who builds the proverbial better mousetrap is liable to run foul of a variety of governmental regulations, or, if he is lucky, be bought out by some conglomerate. He may even find himself offered a franchise to peddle his own product. Similarly, from another direction, an American's individual freedom to work hard is apt to be circumscribed by Trades Union rules.

Somewhere along the line since 1776 the US lost its way. It is no longer the Sweet Land of Liberty that its founders hoped to create. This what is so shattering to sensitive and patriotic Americans. They must either sadly admit that the reality does not conform to the myth or angrily reject as treason any suggestion that this might be so. Either way injury is done to the founders' aspiration of 'one nation, under God'.

6

Missionary Zeal and Manifest Destiny

The record of America's past ventures into international expansionism is an erratic one. There are two distinct themes running concurrently through this area of American history. They may be described as missionary zeal and the Doctrine of Manifest Destiny. Sometimes they harmonized; at others they tended to clash. The essential difference is that the American missionary wishes to spread the word for *its* own sake: the exponent of Manifest Destiny does the same, but for *his* own sake. As the American historian, Frederick Merk, put it: the latter acquired territory to increase the nation's wealth, prestige and power, whereas the former feels it a duty to set an example of democracy and individual liberty. From the receiving end, there may not have been too much difference—as Hawaii's Queen Liliuokalani had cause to know after her overthrow was engineered by the sons of missionaries who had come to her island kingdom to spread the Christian gospel, clothe the heathen and cultivate the pineapple. And make a very great deal of money.

President McKinley asserted as the United States seized the Philippines from Spain that 'no imperialist designs lurk in the American mind'. He was surely sincere. The occupation of Manila was virtually bloodless, the Spanish having sold out their interest in the archipelago for $2 million at the Treaty of Paris in 1898. American troops landed after Admiral Dewey had gone through the motions of shelling the Spanish Fleet into submission without losing a single man. A British Royal Navy squadron under Captain Sir Edward Chichester had obligingly headed off a German fleet under Admiral von Diederichs that had threatened to intervene and spoil an otherwise amiable charade. But the Filipinos, who had already risen up under Emilio Aguinaldo to liberate themselves, were then cheated of the fruits of victory. Their national hero, José Rizal, had died in vain. A savage campaign followed as the 'little brown brothers', as McKinley termed them, were duly subdued in turn. The American leader felt they should be brought the benefits of Christianity, ignoring the fact that they had been Roman Catholics almost 400 years. Their subjugation took several years. In the course of it, General Jacob Smith ordered his troops to kill every male over the age of 10 in the province of Samar and make the place a 'howling wilderness'. He was subsequently court martialled, found guilty and sentenced to be—admonished![1]

It was Manifest Destiny, of course, that led America into the war with Spain in the first place. There was singularly little else to excuse it. The *casus belli* in the public eye was the sinking of the *USS Maine* in Havana Harbour, although it was never proved that any Spaniard actually had a hand in it. The result was Spain's ejection from the old Spanish Main; the technical freeing of Cuba from political dependence on Spain to economic dependence on the United States, and the annexation of Puerto Rico outright. This exploit was followed up by the neat trick of securing 'in perpetuity' sovereign

[1] This episode does not commonly feature in America's school history texts covering the period.

rights to the canal, then already under construction
through the isthmus of Panama, by backing up and
granting instant recognition to a local rebellion of
Colombian citizenry in what was previously a province
of that country in 1903. Thus the Republic of Panama
was created. The presence of a cruiser and a company
of US Marines discouraged Colombia from further
argument. Years later America paid Bogota $25 million
to forget the shabby trick—which, naturally, it has not.
The compelling reason was, of course, strategic. It was
deemed essential for the US to have control of the international waterway. And there were similar strictly
non-imperialist operations in Nicaragua, Haiti and the
Dominica, Guatemala—banana republics all—during
the years that ensued. My point in recalling them is not
so much to criticize—it was, after all, the fashion of the
times—as to throw some light on the schizophrenia that
persists in the American mind on the subject of colonialism and intervention in the affairs of smaller nations.

Some American analysts argue that the war with
Spain was merely an aberration. Others, however, say
that America's drive to the Orient was a logical extension of the concept of the ever-beckoning frontier of the
Golden West. The Caribbean and Latin America as a
whole could properly be regarded as the United States'
backyard—indeed, John Quincy Adams, as President
Munro's Secretary of State, had drafted the famous
Doctrine that was designed to warn off all Europeans
from attempting to encroach into the New World from
his time on.

If that was Manifest Destiny, then presumably Com-
modore Matthew Perry's historic visitations to Tokyo
Bay in 1853 and 1854 with his squadron of black ships,
laden with scientific instruments and mechanical toys
with which to fascinate the Shoguns, could be ascribed

to missionary zeal. Perry's expedition was to open the door to trade. It was to have fantastic consequences. It is credited with awakening Japan from centuries of deep, self-imposed seclusion. It came at a moment when the samurai—petty barons and knights—were restless. The visible technological achievements displayed by the American intruders fomented a spirit of rebellion that was to lead fifteen years later to the overthrow of the Shogunate in the name of the Emperor Meiji. The Japanese genie was out of the bottle and has stayed out ever since—and Japan bids fair to be the Pacific's dominant power before the end of this century.

The Americans approached China later on with similar missionary attitudes uppermost. In some ways during this century their feeling for Asia's sleeping giant, up until the time the Communists defeated Generalissimo Chiang Kai-shek in 1949, resembled that of the Victorian British Empire-builders in India and colonial Africa. While the views of the Chinese, the Indians and the Africans may well have been, in differing degrees, markedly at variance with those of their white guardians or mentors, the latter honestly felt they were doing their duty, sacrificing themselves in faraway lands in order to uplift the backward and Godless. That, to be sure, was the vision Rudyard Kipling wished to impart when he wrote, and addressed to the American people, his verses on The White Man's Burden.

It was their lot, he told them,

... to wait in heavy harness on fluttered folk and wild
—your new caught, sullen peoples, half-devil and half-
child ... Ye dare not stoop to less.

And he warned them sombrely that the price would be

... the blame of those ye better, the hate of those ye
guard that would search your manhood through all the

thankless years, cold, edged with dear-bought wisdom,
the judgement of your peers!

Following the Spanish-American war, a decided distaste for such adventures seemed to develop. It was only interrupted by the relatively brief US intervention in the First World War. Woodrow Wilson's role as a founder of the League of Nations was certainly an expression of missionary zeal, yet it was only too swiftly repudiated by the American electorate. It took another world war to pull Americans back on to the track of their Manifest Destiny. And then, almost two full generations later than he foresaw it, Kipling's prediction was fulfilled. The Marshall Plan and the Truman Doctrine were to see the United States elevated to the functions, willy-nilly, of World Policeman.

7

The Plateau of Empire

The Marshall Plan led ineluctably to the Korean war of 1950, to repel outright Communist aggression. It was possible to interpret this as a purely missionary action, which was just as well since, when the US intervened, public opinion had had little time to undergo the necessary moulding, by giving it a United Nations' cover. This UN endorsement secured for the Americans not only a certain amount of material support—a British Commonwealth division and smaller units from a dozen other countries—but, which was more important, moral backing domestically as well.

With Korea, America decisively changed its views. Attitudes towards colonialism were superseded by a much livelier fear of the spread of Communism by armed force all over the globe. From this point on, America's embroilment in virtually every area of tension in the world was inevitable. Washington's view of France's troubles with Communists in Indochina and Britain's in Malaya switched abruptly once China had fallen to Mao. Great purges were soon to take place in the State Department of all officers who had ever expressed the faintest sympathy for the Chicoms, as the new regime was to be officially designated in Washington. Senator Joseph McCarthy's Investigations sub-Committee was to emerge as a kind of Star Chamber before which strong men quailed. Liberal intellectuals of yesteryear were suddenly depicted as the tools, if not

the actual leaders, of a monstrous Moscow plot to en-
slave mankind. McCarthy found treason everywhere
but, being mentally unbalanced, went too far when he
started attacking men like Dean Acheson and General
Marshall for 'losing' China and being 'soft on Communism'. He nonetheless certainly helped uncover such
security risks as Alger Hiss, a pre-war fellow traveller and
rising young diplomat, who was then trapped into a
conviction on perjury charges by a virtually unknown
Californian Congressman, Richard Nixon. It was subsequently to become fashionable to recall the witch-
hunts with anything but revulsion, but at the time
Senator John Kennedy not only kept quiet about
them but his brother Robert actually served on Mc-
Carthy's staff for a while.

The Korean war got off to a very bad start. The
American field commanders under General MacArthur
—as did the supremo himself— woefully underestimated
the quality of the Communist insurgent forces, and the
US divisions rushed in from soft Occupation duty in
Japan were appallingly green. What started out as a
police action dragged into a war. It came unstuck, militarily speaking, from the moment that MacArthur,
having won it after four months hard fighting, proceeded to overplay his hand, converting victory into
something that came dangerously close to a panic defeat. The North Korean army was totally smashed by
the end of October 1950. Its battered remnants had fled
back across the 38th parallel. MacArthur thought he
saw a chance to reunite North and South Korea. Although this certainly exceeded his United Nations'
brief, he tried to do it. He launched two separate corps
into the attack up either flank of the peninsula, leaving
the centre uncovered. The Chinese Communists not un-
reasonably suspected that the American intended to

press on into Manchuria—he had, after all, made a big show of his friendship for Generalissimo Chiang Kaishek and his rump Nationalist Government in Formosa on the eve of opening his drive on the Yalu River. So they hit back—and in the logical place: slap in the vulnerable centre of the two-pronged advance.

MacArthur lost his nerve at this reversal. His intelligence men began issuing the wildest figures about Chicom strength. Suddenly out of nowhere hordes of Reds were depicted swarming like warrior ants across the bleak snows of the bitter Korean winter. The UN forces pulled back so fast on orders from its prestigious commander in Tokyo that for days on end contact was lost with the supposedly onrushing enemy. It was later revealed that MacArthur had not only wanted to use atomic weapons to save the situation but, more significantly, that he only had the haziest notion of what they could do. He even thought at one point of laying a carpet of radio-active dust the length of the Korean frontier as a sort of atomic Hadrian's Wall—it was never explained how he thought this could have been physically accomplished.

Truman sacked MacArthur for insubordination. It should have been for incompetence. It made him a hero when he returned because no one had ever dared puncture the legend of his military genius created for him by diligent publicity flacks. The truth was that the General was in his dotage. He was succeeded by an excellent soldier, General Matthew Ridgway, who took over a badly demoralized Army, whipped it into shape, and managed to stabilize a line roughly along the 38th parallel dividing the two Koreas. Armistice talks then started. It took another 30 months of bloodshed and 30,000 American lives to reach a stalemate settlement, but no peace—a situation which pertains to this day.

Not surprisingly, the US public got heartily tired of the war as it dragged on. The apostles of Manifest Destiny—then known as the China Lobby and later as Hawks—were frustrated because the Establishment in Washington held out against using the Bomb. The missionaries felt that too high a price was being paid in other directions. This confronted the nation with a dilemma which it resolved by electing as President General Dwight Eisenhower, a father-figure and popular hero from the Second World War, who had been resurrected as first commander-in-chief of the newly re-formed Western Alliance forces in Europe. Ike undertook to bring the boys home, and he did.

Technically, of course, Korea was not a war because it was never formally declared. There were doubts at the time about its strict legality. There was even criticism at the entire operation on moral grounds from people whose anti-Communist credentials were not in question. James Michener, the author, for example, claimed that 'starting with Korea the [American] nation developed a seductive, basically immoral and mistaken doctrine: that we could wage war with our left hand a war in which a few men, chosen at random, sacrificed their lives, while with our right hand we maintained an undisturbed economy in which the fortunate stay-at-homes could frolic and make a lot of money.'

The missionary instinct requires full national commitment to underscore the rightness of any chosen course of military action, especially if it involves the use of conscripts. It is not possible to muster a sense of national commitment for small, undeclared wars, even if out of deference for the American anti-colonial tradition some means are found to dress them up as police actions.

Eisenhower perceived this. So did successive Pentagon Chiefs of Staff. It became a guiding principle of US military policy that never again would Americans get tied down in a conventional land war in Asia. A proliferation of military pacts was then entered into which, on the face of it, seemed to conflict with this position. Eisenhower's Secretary of State, John Foster Dulles, a devoutly religious man, believed Communism could be contained with paper alliances. By the time he had done, America was tied into four multilateral treaties (the Rio Treaty for Latin American defence; NATO, the South East Asian Treaty Organization; ANZUS, with Australia and New Zealand) and four bilateral mutual security pacts (with the Philippines, Japan, Nationalist China and South Korea), plus a major role in CENTO, the Anglo-Turco-Persian-Pakistani 'tier' that supposedly contains the USSR from the south.

One may well ask how in the world the United States could hope to remain disengaged from peripheral wars all over the place with such an array of solemn signatures binding it to precisely the opposite. The answer was, of course, an extension of what was in those simple, far-off days dubbed the 'sword and shield concept'. Dulles promised massive nuclear retaliation would be America's immediate response if the Russians—the Chinese not then being in the nuclear business—breached the phalanx of the great Free World alliance. A global trip-wire had been slung. It was preached as doctrine with great earnestness that all of America's allies could rest absolutely secure in the thought that as long as they did their part by providing the ground forces necessary to act as a screen the length of the Iron Curtain, then if the madmen in the Kremlin ever moved against them, the avenging angel, in the shape of the United States' Strategic Air Command, would come hurtling out of the sky to demolish them with nuclear devastation. By way of lending an extra touch of credibility to this dogma, a considerable American ground force remained assigned to NATO in Europe, as hostages to it. The Massive Retaliation deterrent called for the deployment of long-range bombers, wheeling the skies in relays on constant day and night alert; later it called for the deployment of intercontinental missiles. And soon it became apparent that the only kind of war America would be in any condition to fight was Armageddon. From this chilling realization, doubts began to flow that were to cloud the next two decades.

By the end of the Eisenhower era Americans could look around the world and see what a combination of Manifest Destiny and missionary zeal had led them to. Half the world was dependent on a regular flow of American aid. Dulles' elaborate network of alliances were the non-Communist nations' guarantee of freedom. Yet the US was not widely beloved for either. In less than twelve years the nation's military budget alone had swollen to twice the size of the entire budget for all governmental purposes voted by Congress in 1948. Despite its alarming overtones, Dulles' brinkmanship paid off: martial adventures were avoided. And when Britain and France sought to protect their interests, as they saw them, at Suez in 1956, the Secretary piously sabotaged them. Thus, with the solitary exception of a short-lived military comic opera in the US Marine landings in the Lebanon in 1958, the Eisenhower era was long on talk but short on action—and short, too, on overblown idealism.

8

The Camelot Bubble

As far as the great mass of Americans was concerned, Eisenhower kept them out of trouble without agitating their souls. Had he not been barred from a third term thanks to the action of his own Republicans in imposing a two-term limit in the twilight of Truman's Presidency, he would have been re-elected more as a monarch than as a chief executive. But it was not to be. The Ike interregnum was the pause that refreshed. It was time to be moving on again. At that time Arthur Schlesinger Jr., the son of the Harvard historian and biographer of Roosevelt, was writing: 'The nation's capacity for high-tension political commitment is limited, but there is an inherent cyclical rhythm in our affairs.' He predicted that the moment would be ripe in 1960 for rebellion against the trend. He said that in the 1950s the electorate had asked for 'a period of passivity and acquiescence' and been provided with it. The Man in the Grey Flannel Suit—the Organization Man who conformed—had set the decade's pattern. Schlesinger argued passionately that the pendulum was now swinging back.

America's academic activists of the Schlesinger type are missionary zealots who hanker after power and will do anything to get it so long as they do not have to descend to the hurly-burly of the hustings or the sordid backroom political deals that are unavoidable in the real world. They had an exciting innings in the early days of FDR's New Deal: they longed for another.

John F. Kennedy was a shrewd, ruthlessly ambitious young Senator backed by a vastly wealthy father, Joseph P. Kennedy, a Boston Irishman and a former Ambassador to Britain who aspired to found a dynasty —if only to hit out at the New England WASPs who may have snubbed him in his youth. John F. Kennedy was to be the liberal intelligentsia's new Sun King. By the banks of the Potomac they would establish a New Versailles!

Schlesinger detected a 'psychological ferment and unrest' growing in the country. 'One senses a spreading anxiety and frustration in our society; a confused, inchoate feeling that things aren't going right; a growing boredom with excessive self-congratulation and complacency ... a growing desire to start moving forward as a nation again, to renew our national vision and to clarify our national purposes.'

At the same time, of course, the more conservative inheritors of the Manifest Destiny mantle, along with others more prosaic, were increasingly troubled by such evidences of Russian advances in technology as exemplified by the appearance (in 1957) of Sputnik, the first orbiting satellite. A great hue and cry was set up about the supposed 'Missile gap'. The Soviets were solemnly reported to have outstripped the United States in the development of intercontinental ballistic missiles. They had already caught up with the H-bomb. But now, all of a sudden, it seemed as if they could, and therefore would, given half a chance, 'bury' America. Had not Nikita Khrushchev himself boasted as much? Krushchev dropped that famous remark during his American tour as Eisenhower's guest. What he meant by it was that Communism would outlast capitalism—but that was not how it sounded at the time. Nor were the Democrats ready to let it. Fear of being outclassed in strategic weapons made a splendid election campaign issue and it was used for all it was worth.

In his campaign Kennedy contrived to blend the missionary zeal of the liberals with the yearnings of neo-imperialists. The fierce competitive urge that Americans believed was the secret of their industrial prowess drove them to proclaim to the world that they were top nation. They wanted to reform it, too. Schlesinger was able to combine both strands within himself quite easily. 'The threat of Communism and nuclear war ought to give us a sense of purpose,' he wrote, 'but it doesn't seem to.' The nation was 'waiting for a trumpet to sound.'

America must go all out to catch up with Russian weaponry, he declared. It was disgraceful that 'the richest country in the history of the world ... cannot build up as many ICBMs as the much less affluent Soviet Union.' He harped on the need to 'increase our weapons effort' as well as to bring about a 'moral and political revival'. It was vital, he argued, as the means to pursue a 'vigorous foreign policy' that would 'provide the most exciting and significant outlet for our national creativity'. The missile gap, which was one of the elements that contributed to Kennedy's victory over Nixon, was subsequently discovered to be illusory. It did not matter: Kennedy, and the era of New Frontier rhetoric were launched. The handsome young President was lauded by his entourage as a new Theodore Roosevelt. Activism was the thing! Sweep the cobwebs aside!

As those short 1,000 days of the Kennedy reign opened, the nation exulted to the lofty claims of his inaugural address. 'Let every nation know, whether it wishes us well or ill, that we shall pay any price, bear any burden, meet any hardship, support any friend, oppose any foe to assure the survival and success of liberty. This much we pledge, and more ...' He referred to the 'graves of young Americans around the world', and went on to call a crusade for a 'more fruitful life for all mankind'. And there was much pride taken in the thought that 'only a few generations have been granted the role of defending freedom in its hours of maximum danger ... And so, my fellow Americans, ask not what your country can do for you: ask what you can do for your country!'

While there is no gainsaying that there was a great deal that was attractive about the Kennedy era—and it certainly did much to improve the US image overseas if only because of its peculiar glamour—its principal defect was its overblown rhetoric. It pledged America to more tasks and duties than most Americans had any notion of fulfilling.

The truth is that the Kennedy interlude achieved very little indeed. His most far-reaching act of policy was to commit America to the Vietnam war. His liberal fan club—Theodore Sorensen, who wrote the inaugural speech; John Kenneth Galbraith, the economist; Schlesinger and the rest—have tried to deny this, for it is no longer in style to be for the war; but the evidence is inescapable. Even the denizens of the Camelot-in-exile that clustered first round the widow—until she shattered the image by marrying Aristotle Onassis—then Bobby, until he, too, was killed, and finally Senator Ted Kennedy, admit that the Bay of Pigs was a fiasco. But they blame that muddled CIA effort at unhorsing Castro in Cuba on the Eisenhower administration—an inherited project. That Kennedy could easily have either countermanded it, or pressed it to a successful conclusion, is ignored. They prefer to recall the Cuba missiles crisis of the following year.

Kennedy's finest hour when in the words of his

Secretary of State, Dean Rusk, America and Russia stood 'eyeball to eyeball ... and the other fellow blinked first', was not universally regarded as an American triumph. The Russians either dismantled or never completed missile sites they were constructing in Cuba that would have threatened the US mainland. On the other hand, the Americans also quietly withdrew the medium-range missiles they had installed in Turkey and Italy. As seen from the so-called Third World, Krushchev scored by forcing the US to back down in Turkey and Italy, and by making the 'peace-loving' gesture. Kennedy had also reached a secret understanding with the Russians henceforth to block any further attempts by anti-Castro guerillas to mount operations from American soil to liberate Cuba.

There is no doubt that Kennedy was none too keen about getting embroiled in South East Asia. But he was no dove. In 1962, he rushed a regimental combat team, together with support troops and aircraft, into Thailand, ostensibly as a SEATO exercise, in order to shore up the rapidly crumbling position of the Royal Government in Laos. He would have done more had his Chiefs of Staff not advised him that they could secure Laos by direct US intervention provided they were given authority to employ tactical nuclear weapons. ('They did not realize that to the civilian mind that was like saying they could not do the job,' a highly-placed consultant explained afterwards.)

In Vietnam, despite its having since been represented that Kennedy would never have despatched as many troops as Lyndon Johnson was to later, American involvement rose dramatically from a few hundred advisers and supply personnel to more than sixteen thousand in November 1963. The Pentagon had been directed to draw up plans for the despatch of combat forces.

The sober truth is that two of Kennedy's closest advisers, who later turned against it, played major roles in involving the United States in the Vietnam mess. It was McGeorge Bundy, his special assistant for National Security Affairs, who personally advised Johnson in February 1965 to move in combat troops. Bundy had been sent to find out what was going on. As fate would have it, he was in Pleiku in the Central Highlands at the very moment the Vietcong elected to carry out a raid on a nearby American camp. They killed seven Americans and knocked out a number of helicopters. Bundy thereupon recommended the first air raids against North Vietnam as a reprisal. It so happened that Russia's premier, Alexi Kosygin, was in Hanoi at that very moment, which can hardly have helped cool matters.

Then there was Robert McNamara—hailed by Kennedy as the finest Defence Secretary ever and equally enthusiastically applauded by Johnson later. With monotonous regularity, McNamara guessed wrong in Vietnam. Every time he visited the war zone, he pronounced that the situation was much improved. By the time the US force level had topped the half-million mark, even he was beginning to have doubts. Like Bundy, who earlier made his exit to the Ford Foundation, he began to voice them around Washington to close friends—who whispered it further.

The Kennedy legend-makers had a hard time explaining McNamara until he ducked out of the Pentagon and into the World Bank. But we have not heard the last of his works. He is personally a most likeable man, yet his sweeping decisions as Defence Secretary have produced one disaster after another—all of them extremely expensive—the reverberations of which are likely to last for years to come.

McNamara was formerly president of the Ford Motor Company. He was picked for the Pentagon as an inspired exemplar of all that is held new and shiny in modern management techniques. The churlish pointed out that under his stewardship Ford had produced an appalling dud model; the Edsel. It cost the firm millions in losses before it was discontinued. As Secretary he did re-establish civilian control over the military 'brass', but he also lumbered the American taxpayer with a whole range of super-Edsels.

Against the urgent advice of his Service chiefs, McNamara and his civilian 'systems analysts'—his so-called 'whizz-kids'—insisted on buying the General Dynamics swing-wing fighter-bomber, the F-111. He felt substantial savings could be achieved by producing a plane fit for use by either the Navy or the Air Force. Rival designs might be cheaper in the first instance, but 'commonality' was what he prized. That the makers of the chosen plane should happen to be located in Texas, in an area where it was peculiarly desirable to propitiate the local electorate with the upcoming 1964 elections in mind, was dismissed as an unworthy thought. Nonetheless, for the excellent reason that, as it developed, the machine became so heavy that no aircraft carrier afloat could accommodate it, the Navy finally succeeded in rejecting the F-111. That left the Air Force stuck with it. The RAF would have been, too, had it not been providentially decided, on simple economy grounds, to cancel the British order. Endless defects have shown up since then. The wings fell off in the fifteenth crash. By the time 223 had been delivered, including early models so underpowered as to be incapable of serious combat, the cost per machine had almost quadrupled to $12.7 million.

Under McNamara's aegis, similarly disheartening follies had been perpetrated in a high-speed, armed helicopter, the Cheyenne; in a huge, 800-seat troop-carrier, the C5A Galaxy; in the MBT-70, a joint-production tank venture with the West Germans, and several other projects. Cost overruns had been prodigious in every one—the ultimate irony being that 'cost-effectiveness' was one of McNamara's watchwords. And what is even more astounding has been the revelation that in spite of all the spending, the US Navy's ships today are woefully over-age by comparison with the Russians', while the Air Force complains that, thanks to the F-111 fixation, it lacks an advanced fighter or a bomber. Doubtless by pouring more money into these projects, not all will be written off as a dead loss. But morale has been dented at all levels in the process.

Under Kennedy, too, the defence doctrine was adopted of a 'two-and-a-half war' strategy. In other words, America should be able to stand off China and Russia simultaneously, while leaving enough in reserve to mop up such minor problems as might be presented in the case of a Communist take-over in, say, the Dominican Republic. As a further embellishment to this, the idea was conceived that it was necessary to develop a system of 'flexible response' if any and all wars in which the United States should become embroiled were not automatically to degenerate into the terminal nuclear holocaust. The Dulles doctrine of 'massive retaliation' was quietly dismantled.

The drawback with tinkering with an established precept of strategic theology, as critics of that 'Clausewitz of thermo-nuclear war', Herman Kahn, have noted, is that it makes the unthinkable altogether too thinkable. Kennedy was much influenced by Kahn. And this in turn excuses France's President Charles de Gaulle for calculating that 'flexible response' might well be no response at all—and hence his determination to go it alone and develop a purely French deterrent *force de frappe*. It might never totally annihilate the potential foe, but it was at least arguable that he might feel restrained by the implicit threat: 'I may not be able to kill you, but I'll wrench your arm off before you kill me!'

Having seen how McNamara could vastly discomfit the Anglo-Saxon 'special', if poor, relation by calmly cancelling the Skybolt air-to-ground missile, which would have extended the useful life of the RAF's V-bombers, as well as SAC's B-52s, for another decade, de Gaulle had surely scant reason to repose much faith in the new crew in Washington. The Americans had not even agreed to share nuclear secrets with France, even though she had already let off her first bomb in the Sahara to prove her scientists had progressed far enough to meet the stipulations of the McMahon Act (these would seem to permit such sharing of technical data with a nation that has made 'significant' nuclear progress).

Then the West Germans began to get restive. It was in order to assuage their presumed appetite for nuclear weapons of their own that McNamara's military planners were ordered to dream up a preposterous concept called the Multilateral Force, or MLF, for mixed-manned ships armed with nuclear-armed rockets. It is hard to credit it now, but when this was unveiled at the Pentagon before a bewildered foreign Press corps, the scheme solemnly advanced would have seen Polaris missiles of the type used in nuclear submarines fitted into bogus merchant ships.

When this plan was first unfolded, the walls of the

briefing room were hung with maps showing the world's busiest shipping lanes in swathes of grey of varying widths. It was duly explained by a charming admiral, who later was assigned the task of trotting around the capitals of Europe to try and sell the scheme, that it would be much easier to put crews of mixed nationality into surface ships than submarines. There would be fewer claustrophobic problems arising from the smells of strange cooking, for example. Moreover, on the principle of the Q-ships in the First World War, it seemed a bright idea to make it hard for the Russians to locate the projected NATO missile-carrying vessels by disguising them as ordinary tramp steamers mingling with real ones! By way of illustrating the point, the admiral then turned to a lovingly-made model, fully four feet long, of such a mixed-manned nuclear freighter on his desk. He pressed a hidden button and, piff-bang, a plastic miniature missile flipped to the ceiling from a launch-pad cunningly hidden beneath a cargo hatch.

That it would be wholly illegal under international law to disguise a warship as a merchantman, and particularly in peacetime, had been overlooked. Indeed, the entire mixed-manned surface vessel MLF, along with its variant, the Allied Nuclear Force, or ANF, which Harold Wilson later dreamt up in an attempt to get the Americans out of an absurd impasse, was eventually allowed to die a natural death and swept under the rug. The only reason for recalling it now is to illustrate the fantastically amateurish, *ad hoc* nature of so much of what was labelled by the New Frontier's enthusiastic publicists as Kennedy's 'Grand Design'.

The object of the MLF was to put numerous fingers on the nuclear trigger—although America, naturally, was to retain the safety catch. The theory was that this might result in the Germans, or others, who might doubt the US' resolve to respond to any frontal attack on allied soil, feeling reassured. To give the Germans nuclear weapons of their own seemed clearly out of the question for the simple reason that the Russians would never tolerate it, one was told in background briefings. It only emerged long afterwards that General Curtis Le-May, who was US Air Force Chief of Staff at the time, took precisely the opposite view. He thinks to this day that it would be much better to hand out 'nukes' to every and any ally that wants them on the grounds that they can then all look out for themselves, or even go to war with one another, if they feel they must, without involving the United States in their quarrels. It is certainly safe to say that he was not—and is not—alone in holding this alarming opinion.

The keepers of the Kennedy flame—those who aspire one day to return to power under the leadership of Senator Ted—prefer to forget that such free-wheeling proposals as these were common coinage in the Washington of Jack's day. They do not choose to believe that their hero would have acted in any way but contrary to his elected successor in South East Asia or, for that matter, the Caribbean. Yet the evidence is overwhelming that he had no very clear or fixed philosophy guiding him other than a desire to have and hold power for its own sake. The overwhelming grief that flooded across the nation after Dallas obliterated memory. That the *New York Times* and other liberal periodicals were starting to voice anguished criticisms of Kennedy's failures, as they saw them, in the domestic and foreign fields during the weeks before the tragedy was instinctively forgotten.

What the second-wave Kennedyites chose to remember are things like the Alliance for Progress, as the aid

programme for Latin America was grandiosely entitled, and the Peace Corps. The former has been a
severe disappointment, to say the least. As for the
latter, it has probably done more good to young Americans by giving them a taste of life in exotic backward
lands than it has done their hosts. Its success has been
tarnished in several prickly 'emerging' countries by
charges, whether warranted or not, that the Corps has
been used as a cover for CIA operations.

Had Kennedy not been shot in Dallas, one wonders
how many of the Camelot clan would have survived in
office. For example, John Kenneth Galbraith was
shipped out to New Delhi as Ambassador in order to rid
Kennedy of an amusing friend who could also become
a fearsome liability if let loose amongst orthodox Congressmen in the capital. By 1963, Galbraith was showing
signs of mutiny and trying to return home. Harvard
needed him, he said. Yet on arriving in India two years
earlier, Galbraith betrayed his vast arrogance by an-
nouncing to reporters who greeted him at Palam air-
port: 'As an economist, this is my St Crispin's Day.' To
make sure they did not miss the point, his remarks were
distributed in a hand-out by his press officer. The Indians were not at all sure that the tall, gangling professor was in order in assigning himself the role of Henry
V and they wondered whose Agincourt he thought he
was about to direct.

Galbraith today basks in a reputation as a man of
public affairs rather than as a witty writer of rather glib
economic journalism, because of that Ambassadorship.
The truth is that he never had the slightest influence
on Nehru—an even more arrogant man—except in instances when it suited the Indian. He failed to dissuade
Nehru from invading Goa. Nehru crossed him up by
taking a tortuously neutral line over the 1961 Berlin

crisis. Only when the Indians were given a nasty scare by the Chinese in the Himalayas were they quick to accept US arms aid—but slower to acknowledge it with public thanks, preferring to reserve those for the Russians. If Galbraith had since forgotten the whole experience and slunk back quietly to the groves of academe, one could dismiss his bumblings as a joke. But the trouble is, typical of his kind, he hankers after political limelight yet. He is the elected leader of the liberal ginger group, Americans for Democratic Action, and as such is more than merely sighing for the triumphal return of the Young Pretender.

It is men like him—scores of intellectual valets who once served at the Kennedy Court—who have turned Kennedyism into a mystical force, a rallying point for woolly-minded idealists and plain buccaneers of every stripe or none, that would probably startle either of the slain and sometimes seem to bewilder the last of the Kennedy line. What has to be said today is that Kennedyism had little substance. Its designs were less grand than erratic. It blew a bubble of expectancy in the US that had to burst. Kennedy had many of his people dreaming the impossible dream. It is from this that, in the late 1960s, they painfully awoke into a deeper disillusion than they would have been plunged into if the afflatus of idealism had never overwhelmed them.

It was Vietnam, above all, that brought about this awakening.

9

Vietnam and its Consequences

The biggest single casualty in Vietnam has been America's self-esteem. The realization that even the world's most powerful nation could not subdue a small, sub-tropical agrarian people like the North Vietnamese and crush the Communists in South Vietnam was a really bitter blow. Had President Johnson's advisers in the spring of 1965—virtually all of them carryovers from the Kennedy era—foreseen the war continuing five and more years longer, it is hard to believe they would have fallen in with the adventure.

The pivotal decision to move in combat troops—US Marines—to protect American supporting units behind the hitherto purely South Vietnamese military effort was taken in February 1965, following McGeorge Bundy's on-the-spot recommendation. And this led remorselessly to Johnson's statement of July 28: an open-ended commitment of America's resources to the 'different kind of war'.

The 'central fact', as he then put it, was that North Vietnam 'spurred by Communist China' had as its goal the conquest of the South, and the 'defeat of American power' in order to 'extend the Asiatic dominion of Communism'. 'There are great stakes in the balance,' he went on, arguing that if America was 'driven from the field ... then no nation can ever again have the same confidence in our promise of protection. In each the forces of Independence would be weakened. And an

Asia so threatened by Communist domination would imperil the security of the United States itself ... we did not choose to be the guardians at the gate. But there is no one else!' He went on to draw the Munich analogy that 'success only feeds the appetite of aggression', winding up with the pledge: 'We will not surrender and we will not retreat.'

From that moment on, American manpower and material began pouring into what seemed like a bottomless quagmire. Two years later it was computed that it cost $234,000 to kill a single Communist regular. Three years later, the figures showed the war's annual cost was half as much again as the *entire* British budget. For a public reared on 'Superman' comic books and 'Batman' strips where the Good Guys have only, in the final analysis, to press a button and, 'P-o-w!', the Bad Guy disintegrates, the reality was painfully disturbing.

It would, however, be quite incorrect to assume that there were serious moral doubts about the propriety of the Vietnam intervention at the outset. These were not to manifest themselves until much later. It was not until the number of Americans actually ashore in the war zone rose beyond the 200,000 mark that dissent became a phenomenon. Beyond that figure it became impossible to disguise the fact that conscripts would be required in increasing numbers to flesh out the ranks. As long as actual combat could be confined to predominantly regular volunteer units, political backlash against the war was minimal. It was only when the children of more articulate sectors of the community began to find themselves caught up in the Vietnam draft that opposition began to grow vociferous.

The public opinion polls consistently showed hawks outnumbered doves in America as a whole until well after Johnson had bowed out. There was considerable sympathy for the view that the Texan was forcing the military to fight the war 'with their hands tied'. At the height of his prestige, General William Westmoreland, the theatre commander, told a New York audience: 'It's going to be a question of putting maximum pressure on the enemy anywhere and everywhere that we can. We will have to grind him down. In effect, we are fighting a war of attrition, and the only alternative is a war of annihilation, which I think we have ruled out as a matter of policy.' Westmoreland seemed somewhat put out that the latter should be so. The simple solution of 'creating a desert and calling it peace'—Tacitus' description of Roman strategy in Britain—was denied him. As a serving soldier, he accepted it. But not so General Curtis LeMay, who, having retired, was free to urge that North Vietnam should be 'bombed back into the stone age'.

Most Americans at the time agreed with the big stick approach. This was amply demonstrated in the summer of 1966 when Johnson ordered the bombing of Hanoi and Haiphong's oil dumps for the first time. The effect was immediate where it counted—and that was not in Vietnam but back in the US. In the expectation that the decision would shorten the war, the President's rating in the Gallup Poll shot up from the low 40s to the mid-50s in percentage terms overnight.

The Louis Harris survey further showed then that 86 per cent of American voters confidently believed that bombing would hasten the end of the war, against 14 per cent who suspected it would stiffen the enemy's resolve to fight on.

'The picture', I wrote at the time from Saigon, 'is very different in Vietnam. Whether the latest escalation was well timed or not is hardly worth discussing and belongs in a geo-political context that seems remote from present reality on the ground here. And this is that whatever Americans may think back home, out here they know they are stuck into a war that their generals expect to go on for a very long time indeed— ten years at least—and get much bigger.

'The fact is that the Americans are not winning yet. All that has happened is that they are not losing. And it is hard to see how, militarily, they can. But that is not the same thing at all. If Johnson had not taken the plunge (in 1965) and committed US troops directly to South Vietnam's war effort, universal opinion here is that Saigon's resistance would by now have collapsed. The Vietcong "had it made", as Americans say. This is no longer the case: they have been held. But the price has been that of turning the whole affair into an American war. While it may be deemed convenient in Washington to describe it as an effort in support of a brave people embattled by aggressive Communist in-filtrators, and how all that is required is for Hanoi to "come to the conference table", this fools no one here.'

I went on to describe the enormous build-up in American and allied manpower, pointing out that these things have a way of creating a momentum of their own. Huge new harbour installations were being run up at Cam Ranh Bay, along with new airfields and 10,000-foot run-ways for B-52s. 'Such military secrecy as one might ex-pect to be maintained about the scale and scope of these activities is consistently and continually "blown" by the vast hordes of camp followers converging on the scene. One consortium of American consulting engineers (Brown, Root, Morrison-Knudsen—Brown being a per-sonal friend and campaign contributor to Johnson) al-ready employs 50,000 and expects to hire half as many again. Construction contracts extending into the mid-70s are common talk from Honolulu to Singapore wherever eager entrepreneurs congregate. Saigon itself is bursting with such non-military Americans as contractors' foremen, motor car salesmen, insurance agents and stockbrokers chasing the GI dollar.'

Saigon was also full then of 'spooks'—intelligence agents of every kind, including the ubiquitous CIA. The overpowering presence of so many Americans in and out of uniform was scarcely conducive to 'winning the hearts and minds' of the people. Psychological warfare specialists were the first to admit this. An old Vietnamese friend I had known since the French days remarked sourly that 'in the old days, we were at least second-class citizens. Now we have been demoted to tenth!' Whereas I, as a Caucasian, would be courteously treated by American military policemen, he was barked at. The resentments thus created were obviously easy for the Communists to exploit. The orthodox military mind seemed incapable of coping with the problem and it took literally years to thin out the preposterously heavyweight 'tail' of rear echelon units, supply and communications troops, that sprawled all over the overcrowded capital and shift most of them to new camps upcountry.

There were American political warfare experts who knew perfectly well that Westmoreland's massive search-and-destroy strategy, with its emphasis on mobility and firepower was, as one of them put it, 'like trying to swat a mosquito in the dark with a sledgehammer'. But they quickly lost hope of being able to do anything about it. They had the hot breath of Washington demanding results down the backs of their necks all the time. General Ed Lansdale, the original model for Graham Greene's *Quiet American,* would candidly parry any question about how his 'psy-war' effort was going with: 'If you've come from Washington, you can tell me: that's where the action is!' The need to produce statistics and other quotable evidence of progress to keep the American public happy, particularly with elections forthcoming, continually inhibited realistic planning.

It was precisely because the White House demanded a quick solution that the South Vietnamese were elbowed aside. The Americans insisted on doing the job themselves, believing that they could do it faster that way than by training the natives. That guerilla warfare might have rules of its own seldom worried ebullient new arrivals. Their view was summed up for me in the words of an airborne battalion commander, thus: 'OK! So you may be right we can't win this type fight our way. All I'll say, then, is we're going to change it into the type we can!' He was killed later in a helicopter accident.

It is axiomatic of military affairs that the tactics of the previous war are those that commend themselves first to commanders. The US regular army is led by men who made their reputations in Europe in 1943-45, or in Korea (1950-53). Its senior officers are notoriously suspicious of such new-fangled innovations as the Green Beret counter-insurgency specialists. Americans fought shy of Commando-type units during the Second World War. There is a deep-seated feeling that élitism should be avoided.

Not unnaturally, the South Vietnamese armed forces, which had, incidentally, been trained and equipped with obsolescent US weapons and techniques by an American military mission since the French departed in 1954, were not unhappy to see their mentors move in to bear the brunt of the fighting. Their casualties declined markedly as those of the Americans rose. The destruction continued. The bomb tonnage dropped on the countryside was soon to surpass that let loose over all Europe in the Second World War. Westmoreland's headquarters—Pentagon East—spread and spread. Serried banks of computers were installed to produce instant information on the state of the game: Hamlet Evaluation Statistics (HES), body counts, kill ratios, vehicle sightings on the Ho Chi Minh trail. The jungle on the mountainous Cambodian and Lao borders seemed to have been sewn with electronic sensors to keep watch on infiltrators. Newer and nastier antipersonnel bombs were tried; great tracts of rubber plantation and other vegetation were laid waste by defoliants.

As the whole sorry business dragged on, more and more objections began being raised back home as to the initial premises upon which the intervention was based. These in turn had a debilitating effect on morale—and not least on the morale of the South Vietnamese non-Communists. It was just what Hanoi had hoped and planned for. The Americans might not be militarily defeatable in the field, but there seemed an excellent chance of goading them into defeating themselves at home. Inevitably there was an interreaction between the growing malaise in Washington and that in Saigon. Senator William Fulbright's Foreign Relations Committee hearings developed into a regular Star Chamber inquisition of Johnson's policymakers. They had little effect beyond creating eddies of mistrust and confusion, as reflected in bickerings between the soldier-politicians of Saigon, the Buddhists and the Catholics, the sects and, in short, everyone who had reason to worry about what might happen if the US bolted.

The crunch finally came with the Communists' lunar new year—or Tet—offensive in February 1968. The North Vietnamese and Vietcong struck very hard in a series of well-coordinated attacks against almost every major town in the country. In Saigon itself a suicide squad managed to penetrate the American Embassy.

Ferocious fighting ensued.

In fact, although it was not immediately appreciated, the attackers took such tremendous losses in this spectacular operation, they almost succeeded in knocking themselves out. They had evidently hoped and expected that the civilian population would rally to them and against the Americans and their 'lackeys'. This did not occur. Unfortunately, however, General Westmoreland, who had only recently been back in Washington at Johnson's behest to deliver morale-boosting speeches about how well the war was going, failed to counterpunch. He was slow to realize that in order to mount their assault on Saigon in particular the enemy had thrown in virtually everything they had, which left their rear vulnerable to the Americans in a way it would seldom be again.

Westmoreland had no feel for the overriding political objective: winning the allegiance of the South Vietnamese to the Saigon Government. For him the whole country was a huge sand-table battlefield. Yet he muffed the one chance he ever had to pull off a set-piece envelopment of the enemy as their shock troops reeled back from what had proved to be an abortive offensive. The main reason for this was that he did not trust the intelligence supplied him in advance by the South Vietnamese, and then, once the Communist attack had started, he was scared lest the population would rise up precisely the way the enemy had hoped it would.

The Tet offensive came hard on the heels of the North Korean seizure of the ill-fated spy ship *USS Pueblo* off Wonsan in January—an ignominious episode revealing the powerlessness of America to cope with midget enemies that shook Washington badly. The anti-war movement was now very much on the march. The anguish voiced by youthful pacifists grew steadily louder as time went by. The various methods by which better-off youngsters could dodge conscription by student deferments began to exhaust themselves. Then serious objections began to be raised on Wall Street. The most powerful financial community in the nation, not to say the world, began to cast grave doubts on the wisdom of continuing the war. The prestigious *Wall Street Journal* came right out and said so.

Not even the US economy could stand guns *and* butter on the scale the Vietnam imbroglio was now requiring. For political reasons in 1966, Johnson had hesitated to call for any extra taxes. He had the mid-term Congressional elections in mind. Hence the Pentagon's budget had to be discreetly fudged in 1967. Then Congress developed a marked reluctance to vote a surtax to help pay for the war—or ward off inflation, which was the other way of putting it—so that heavy borrowings had to be made on a tightening money market. If the war had been quickly won, the problem of paying for it would still have arisen but the bills could have been met by post-dated cheques on future revenues which would—it was hoped—continue to rise. But now the prospect of an early end to the continuing drain seemed dim.

It was precisely at this moment that Westmoreland chose to deliver to General Earl Wheeler, Chairman of the Joint Chiefs of Staff, who was rushed out to fact-find, his request for yet another 206,000 men on top of the 510,000 already assigned him. That would have necessitated the calling up of another 400,000 to active service at a cost of a further $10,000 million a year on top of the $2,500 million a month Vietnam was already costing. The demand ensured Westmoreland's removal—he was kicked upstairs soon afterwards.

Westmoreland's motives in making his extravagant and, for him, final demand for more manpower may have sprung from a deep yearning he shared with his brother professionals for 'legitimacy'. He knew well that 206,000 men could not be provided without declaring a state of national mobilization. This would mean, in effect, a declaration of war. And that would require the home front to come out solidly behind its men in the field on a my-country-right-or-wrong basis. For morale reasons that relate peculiarly but directly to the American tradition of the 'citizen army', a tradition which goes back to the foundation of the Republic, it galls West Point products of Westmoreland's type to be regarded in any way as mercenaries. This goes hand in hand with their dislike for unconventional units like the Green Berets. It also explains a strange reluctance to press for an all-regular service on the philosophic-historic grounds that empires which come to rely on professional legionaries to do their fighting are on the way to decay.

The net effect of the post-Tet request for further reinforcement was to jolt Johnson into the realization that some other way out of the Vietnam mess had to be found. It was certainly this more than the emergence of Senator Eugene McCarthy at the head of the 'dump LBJ' children's crusade in the first of the election year's primaries in New Hampshire that led him to withdraw from contention as candidate for re-election. He remained convinced he could have won against Nixon, or any other Republican, in November: but he accepted that Hanoi would never reach a compromise settlement with him. He felt, therefore, that he had to prove his sincerity in wishing to make peace before worse disaster struck.

Johnson's admirers have since claimed—and not without justice—that he was singularly ill-served by his advisers whom he inherited from Kennedy. His aim and object in Vietnam and Asia generally was to spread the boon of his Great Society—the name he gave his Administration on being elected in his own right in 1964—to the brown, yellow and black folks of the underdeveloped world. He had a vision of the Mekong River, for example, being tamed and tapped for electric power and irrigation on a vast scale—just as was his own beloved Pedernales in East Texas under FDR. As a onetime schoolteacher to poor Mexicans, he thrilled to the idea of installing educational television worldwide by satellite.

At the highwater mark of American Empire—before the self-styled 'Guardian at the Gate' wearied of the role—Johnson's triumphal Asian tour of 1966 convinced him, and others, that he would go down in history as the great white father who saved Asia for freedom. Once the war was done, he pledged America to promote vast new economic uplift projects to repair the ravages of war in Vietnam for friend and foe. He launched the new Asian Development Bank and encouraged further regional co-operative efforts. What Marshall meant to post-war Europe, Johnson would to the Orient: it was no petty ambition, nor despicable.

Yet when the moment of truth arrived it must be recorded that the ranks of his earlier counsellors had thinned considerably. Only Dean Rusk, his Secretary of State, and Walt Rostow, Special Assistant for National Security Affairs, stood firm, if wrong-headedly beside him to the end. McNamara was on his way out before Tet but had not actually left office when the Communists struck. His successor, Clark Clifford, the behind-the-scenes adviser to every president since Truman, then shocked Johnson by switching abruptly from hawk to dove after taking over. McGeorge Bundy, Cyrus Vance and Douglas Dillon all made the about-face to recommend de-escalation, too. The venerable Averell Harriman, his special envoy at the Paris peace talks and once a staunch advocate of a firm line, had already gone soft. But the clincher, it subsequently emerged, was Dean Acheson.

Acheson, the leading elder statesman in Washington and above all the surviving architect of the Marshall Plan and all that went with it in America's assumption of world leadership, was the one man alive who could halt a further expansion of the Vietnam effort. He had long supported the war. I had myself been bellowed at by Acheson for an entire dinner at his own table for once daring to suggest that American tactics in Vietnam were not conducive to the successful prosecution of a highly political civil war, and that the excessive use of firepower was liable to alienate at least as many peasants as it converted. Acheson had been very indignant and even went so far as to suggest that my reservations about the effectiveness of US policy in the war were due to my British decadence. Against such a background of conviction on the part of Acheson I can imagine how Johnson must have felt when he told him after Tet: 'With all due respect, Mr President, the Joint Chiefs of Staff don't know what they're talking about.' Two weeks later, after delving further at Johnson's direct request, and cross-examining a wide range of key but second echelon officials, he reported back bluntly to the President that the Joint Chiefs had 'led him down the garden path' and Westmoreland's demands simply could not be met at a price worth paying.

As these defections gradually became known outside the White House inner circle, which did not happen all at once, the American in the street could be excused for feeling as disconcerted as a passenger in a transatlantic airliner might on learning suddenly from the stewardess that the pilot was drunk, the navigator had fallen overboard and the radio-operator was on a methadrine trip. It is, after all, natural for the average man to assume that his leaders and established elders know what they are doing. It has come as a traumatic shock to learn, by their own admission, that this was not actually the case.

After Tet and Acheson's report, the idea of a battlefield victory was effectively ruled out. The war ground on miserably but simply as a holding operation punctuated by efforts to extract at the negotiating table in Paris some settlement short of a total sell-out of South Vietnam. Whether a ceasefire could have been achieved by relaxing pressure further, as some argued, was surely highly problematic. The ultimate irony was that it had now fallen to Richard Nixon, the Republican who owed his election in great measure to his promise to extricate the nation from Vietnam, to take whatever credit is going for finishing off the job. And in 1970 it began to look as if it was going to finish him off instead.

Since June 1969, when Nixon conferred with Saigon's President Thieu at Midway in the Pacific, the process had got under way of withdrawing American troops and 'Vietnamizing' the fighting. Responsibility for fighting their own war was being returned to the principals. The United States, as a matter of high policy, intended from here on to take a back seat in Asia post-Vietnam. This was the Nixon Doctrine as spelled out to those of us who accompanied him on his tour of Asian capitals later that summer. The 'guardian at the gate' concept of only four years previously had totally vanished. On the contrary, the new message was that the US could not act as world policeman and had no intention of doing so.

The only exception to that general rule would be in a case where a nuclear threat was involved. Nixon was quite precise on the point: the time had come, he said, for the US to be emphatic that it would, first, stand by its existing treaty obligations, and secondly, encourage the Asian nations themselves to handle their own problems—should no nuclear power be involved.

It should be noted that the SEATO pact, under which America was bound to assist Thailand, was carefully vague about what its signatories were expected to do in the event of externally-directed subversion. And this, rather than frontal attack, had become the accepted *modus operandi* in Asian conflicts. The likelihood of China invading the Philippines when it had yet to oust the Nationalists from Formosa did not seem very menacing. And America had made it clear that she was certainly not going to get mixed up in small wars between neighbours—such as between Malaysia and the Philippines over Sabah.

Nixon was keen also to normalize relations gradually with Communist China. The Johnsonian notion that China 'spurred on' Hanoi in Vietnam to defeat American power in the interest of 'expanding the dominion of Communism' likewise faded. Nixon's view was that China should not be permanently excluded from the comity of nations. Whereas it might once have been true that Mao Tse-tung's brand of Communism was dangerously alluring to the rising generation in many newly independent nations emerging from colonialism, today this was probably no longer the case. If any one country in Asia had the capacity beyond others to act as an inspiration, it was surely Japan. Japan's gross national product had outstripped that of China with seven times the population. Indeed, virtually all the peoples of the non-Communist Asian States were faring better than the Chinese economically, Nixon argued.

The US could not roll back its defences entirely from

the Pacific, of course. It was a Pacific power by virtue of geography. But in future this power was to be less blatantly deployed. The new-look strategy for America is couched in terms like 'low profile', 'soft options', 'hulldown over the horizon'. Washington is to eschew overweaning paternalism for a more discreetly avuncular posture. Overseas outposts and garrisons are to be cut. Above all: no more Vietnams! And not too much zeal.

It is scarcely surprising that many of the Asian leaders began to display a distinct edginess as word percolated through to them from their Washington envoys of this seeming turnaround. But, on the whole, they got the message straight. The American line was that by standing firm in Vietnam in 1965, time had been gained for the non-Communists to gain a firmer hold on neighbouring countries that might have fallen like the proverbial dominoes. Indonesia was cited as the prime example of one where the tide had been turned—the local Communist party (PKI) had been wiped out, with considerable bloodshed, to be sure. Whether that would last or not remained to be seen, but it had at least demonstrated that the Maoists were not inevitably the wave of the future.

Nixon had uncomfortable moments during the autumn of his first year in office (1969) as a result of huge anti-war demonstrations staged in Washington and other cities around America. It must surely have inspired the hope in Hanoi that the US was on the point of cracking on the home front—just as the French did after the battle of Dien Bien Phu in 1954. The Communists may well have thought the same of the Cambodian sanctuaries sweeps which caused even deeper domestic consternation in America in 1970. A great impatience welled up across the country because the Paris peace talks remained deadlocked and blunder succeeded blunder in the field. It was all too easy for the idealistic, liberal youngsters of the New Left to see Nixon as the villain supporting the odious Thieu in Saigon. In their anxiety to be rid of the mud of Vietnam, nothing short of an instant American exit—a physical impossibility —would satisfy them. And as one White House official remarked crossly: 'They don't just want us to quit. They want us to deliver Thieu's head on a silver salver to the Vietcong as well!'

By the end of 1969, the thunder on the Left was subsiding. It welled up again the following May as the fighting spilled from Vietnam into the Cambodian sanctuaries. How long this see-sawing would continue plainly depended on the unpredictable behaviour of the enemy rather than to America's staying power. Incredibly, however, there were signs that 'Vietnamization' was having a sobering effect on Saigon. Once it was realized the US withdrawal had been irreversibly decided on, the régime saw it was a case of swim or sink. But the risk always remained that the Communists might make some move that would either delay the winding down of the war, or worse still, produce another crisis situation to which America would have to react or admit undisguised and ignominious defeat. This, in turn, could lead to an angry reaction within the US. But there was, too, always the danger of the unexpected leading to fresh entanglements—as the Cambodian affair proved.

There is also the problem looming of the returning centurion. Americans having been brought up to believe that they have never lost a war do not take kindly to the idea. If defeat should be brought home to them too harshly, and if the realization of defeat was accompanied by unpleasantnesses, such as unemployment, a slump, a breakdown of law and order, race riots, and so on, then the consequences could be grave. Already there is a morale problem in the Pentagon. Vietnam has had a depressing effect on regular recruiting. The prestige of the uniformed services has suffered from scandals over kick-backs in NCO clubs. Then there were the Pinkville massacre stories, which hurt not so much because atrocities occurred as because of a seeming chain of command failure and a breakdown in discipline. On top of that have come economy drives and Congressional rows about soaring costs in weapons development. All these things have produced a rash of resignations amongst brighter officers, who can earn more money outside, and a slowdown in re-enlistments.

Worse than all of this is the echo of the complaint of Marcus Flavinius, a centurion writing back to Rome from Outer Gaul in the 1st century:

'We were told on leaving our native soil, Cousin Tertellus, that we were going to defend the sacred rights and benefits brought by us to populations in need of our assistance and our civilization. We were able to verify this was true. We shed our youth and our blood and regretted nothing. But I am told that in Rome factions and conspiracies are rife and that many people talk of abandonment and vilify what we have wrought. I cannot believe this to be true. Make haste to reassure me, I beg you, and tell me that our fellow citizens understand us and support the glory of the Empire as we do. But if it should be otherwise, and if we have left our bleached bones in these deserts in vain, then beware, O Tertellus, beware of the anger of the Legions!'

Marcus Flavinius' bitterness is duplicated in many an American officers' mess in Vietnam today.

The real tragedy about Vietnam, leaving aside the whole question of whether it was the right war at the right time and the right place or not, is the way it has split America. As Nixon put it, the only people who could defeat America were the Americans themselves —but when he said it, they had, in effect, done so. The inability of so cumbersome and wasteful a military machine as theirs to cope with guerilla warfare; the arrogance and inflexibility of commanders who won their spurs in Europe and then failed to adapt to the different ground rules Asia imposes; the bungling bureaucracy and, not least, the wholesale corruption, blatant profiteering and sheer thievery that character-ized the entire Indochina mess, was altogether too much to sustain patriotic conviction at home.

But for Vietnam, it is doubtful whether America's nihilistic New Left would have been able to make the kind of headway it has since the election year of 1968. It is equally certain, however, that a strong reaction is coming to both the excesses of the militant radicals and to the simple fact of defeat.

Add to this discontent a very strong possibility of a domestic recession, the prospect of embittered soldiers returning home to unemployment, and the outlook is alarming. A disproportionate number of Negroes served in rifle battalions and learnt to shoot to kill. This alone promises to supply an explosive ingredient of its own to future tensions in America's ghettoes. While the fighting in Vietnam was at its height, it used to be claimed that race relations within the US forces in the field underwent an inspiring transformation. Unhappily, this has not lasted: black-white riots have lately be-come a major service problem.

In the testing days ahead, the temptation to turn to authoritarian solutions as an alternative to chaos may be irresistible. Middle America is already turning sharp Right—and inwards. The storm signals are up.

10

Turning Right and Turning Inwards

Nixon entered the White House in January 1969 as the quintessence of middle-class, middle-income America: the champion, as he sees it, of the 'silent majority' of the non-black, non-young, non-trendy and non-poor: the people who go to Church most Sundays, pay up their mortgages, agonize over their incomprehensible children, worry about inflation, the rising crime rate, drug addiction, pornography, and detest the Vietnam war but find it hard to face losing it. They were fed up with race riots. The gold drain perplexed them. Foreigners seemed to be losing respect for the dollar. It had, surely, been different under Eisenhower—and here was Nixon, blessed by Ike from his sickbed and with the national father figure's grandson, David, betrothed to his daughter, Julie. His nomination had taken place at the Republican convention at Miami Beach—the archetype of all that is most stridently vulgar about affluent suburban America and its values, a man-made redoubt constructed of neon, concrete and polyethelyne on sand, isolated from uglier realities by a polluted lagoon. America was tired and fretful—not least of all about her world role.

In public, Nixon naturally talked about 'making the American dream come true' and foreseeing a day when 'America is once again worthy of its flag ... of respect.'

But underlying the tub-thumping was a hard core of realism: he had shelved any idea of 'winning' a military victory in Vietnam. In private—and before he was nominated—he was amazingly candid about it. At a closed session of party delegates, which was surreptitiously tape-recorded by the *Miami Herald* at the time, he let the cat out of the bag. Someone had asked him, he said, if he thought the war was lost. 'I said that if I believed that I won't say it. The moment we say the war is lost you're not going to be able to negotiate, you see. The only way ... is to convince the enemy you've some strength left.' He then went on to claim he would get out of Vietnam the way Eisenhower had from Korea —by negotiating and making the South Vietnamese strong enough to permit a US withdrawal. And 'regarding the future, there won't be any more Vietnams!' he promised.

Similarly, Nixon unveiled his intention to duck the world policeman commitment. He was most warmly applauded when he talked about getting the Allies to share the load 'so we don't fight their wars for them'. As for Russia, he was for telling its leaders that as neither they nor the US wanted nuclear war so the time had come to negotiate. 'We've got to broaden the canvas from Vietnam—they have no reason to end that war. It's hurting us more than them,' he said. 'But we could put the Mideast on the fire. And you could put Eastern Europe on the fire. And you could put trade on the fire. And you could put the power (sic) bombs on the fire ... and you say: "Now, look here. Here's the world. Here is the United States. Here's the Soviet Union. Neither of us wants nuclear war ... They want something else, but they don't want war." So they'll say: "What are we going to do in order to reduce these tensions?"' There was, needless to say, not a word about keeping the Allies informed in any of this.

Nixon's vision sharply differed from that heroic Camelot-by-the-Potomac of the Kennedy era. It was a vision unlikely to charm the young, the poor and the black, who remained a minority in this land for all the noise they made. America suddenly seemed middle-aged, having reached that condition in record-breaking time, compressing British imperial experience of a century following Trafalgar into not much more than a couple of decades. The nation was quietly throwing in the sponge. The Democratic Party Convention in Chicago of 1968 saw Nixon's opponents locked in bitter battle over the Vietnam issue. Nixon himself was already determined to withdraw from Vietnam as rapidly as he could. There were no longer any hawks in the running —only variants of doves. Even the third party candidate, former Alabama Governor George Wallace, while picking General Curtis LeMay as his running-mate, took very good care to insist that he felt America should never have got into the war in the first place and that he, too, would never keep 'American boys' over there indefinitely. The plain, unvarnished truth was that the nation wanted to get out of Vietnam. There was no longer the faintest echo anywhere of Kennedy's famous pledge, 'We shall pay any price, bear any burden, meet any hardship ... to assure the survival of liberty.' Nor was anyone for carrying on as Johnson's 'guardians at the gate'.

What occurred at Chicago, therefore, was a 'happening' that could have easily been avoided. The spectacular collisions between Mayor Richard Daley's police riot squads and demonstrators outside the Hilton Hotel, where both Vice-President Hubert Humphrey and Senator Eugene McCarthy were headquartered, were pure guerilla theatre, along with the sideshow riots in

Grant Park and elsewhere. They were a way of letting off steam. It was plain enough that the militant activists of the emerging New Left—the Mobilization Against the War in Vietnam, or Mobe, and the Youth International Party, the Yippies, were spoiling for trouble. They wanted to prove that the whole System was rotten, and that the only thing to do was tear it down. Theirs was the 'politics of confrontation'. As a studied insult to their elders, the Yippies nominated a pig named Pigasus for the Presidency of the United States. National flags were burned. Communist flags were brandished.

By making common cause for the moment with the frustrated McCarthyite youngsters, they calculated that they, too, would become imbued with hatred for the cops as 'fascist pigs', 'enemies of the people', 'baby burners'—to cite a few milder epithets employed—and become converts to the revolution. When the police behaved badly in their turn, which was entirely predictable in a force that is notable for indiscipline and corruption even by American standards, the young nihilists and their allies were delighted and exultant. Public sympathy swung to the side of the police, which shook liberal commentators to the core. As something of a connoisseur of civil disturbance, I reckon the mayor muffed it. Had Daley and his police chief had the wit, they would have profitably permitted the motley demonstration on the main day of the Convention to march on the hall in the Chicago stockyards, as its organizers wished to. It was a hot and sticky August day. The distance was some five miles. Moreover, the route would have taken the long-haired collegiate and predominantly middle- and upper-middle-class pacifists, with their outrageous slogans and North Vietnamese flags, right through an area of the city that is largely inhabited by working class 'ethnics' who tend towards super-patriotism. Unlike the affluent, the children of these folk have enjoyed less opportunity to dodge conscription for Vietnam by extending their education year after year and securing student deferments. These were Daley's people. They are the sort that hang out the Stars and Stripes from their front porches. Had the Yippies and the Mobe led the Minnesota Senator's children through their streets, the scenario would have been rather different: Chicago's police would have appeared on the nation's (and the world's) televison screens protecting the misguided offspring of the over-privileged from the righteous wrath of the less so.

As it was, the police went berserk. They cracked not only demonstrators over the head but onlookers as well. I myself had my arm broken when a helmeted lunatic clubbed me as I watched Winston Churchill and Jamie Auchinloss—both reporters on the scene and scarcely militant radicals—rescuing a young girl from a plainclothes man who was lunging at her with a billy club at least 100 yards from the main mêlée. The girl, we discovered, was not even a McCarthy supporter—she was for Nixon—but that made no difference. As far as Daley's boyos were concerned, it was open season on the young and any who might be presumed to sympathize with them.

More serious than the mayhem on Chicago's streets —and far more damaging to the Democrats—were Daley's strong-arm tactics inside the Convention hall. He packed the stands with supporters, harassed anti-Humphrey delegates and tinkered with the public address system to gag them. It was all so blatant, the Republicans were overjoyed. Nixon was reputedly beaten in 1960 largely because Daley's well-greased party machine in Cook County carried the day for Kennedy by wholesale fraud, stuffing ballot boxes and generally

rigging the vote in the time-honoured way. This practice is—or was—an accepted feature of Chicago life,
as in other big American cities, even if it is slowly dying
out. Daley wanted Senator Edward Kennedy, as a fellow Irishman, to run: when he would not do so, he
transferred his loyalty reluctantly to Humphrey.

The uproar at Chicago was both a cause and effect
of the growing alienation of America's brightest youngsters. Long before Chicago one began to encounter the
phenomenon of 'turned off' American student youth.
Even as McCarthy's children's crusade was in full
swing, I met angry young SDS (Students for a Democratic Society) adherents who regarded the adopted
leader of the anti-Johnson movement as a fake. They
would tell one without equivocation that in their view
American society was so hopeless that nothing would
do but to scrap the entire 'power structure', McCarthy
included. When asked what they would wish to see
replace it, they would reply that any attempt to answer
that question must of necessity 'institutionalize' the
revolution, which would mean creating another 'power
structure' that would be as bad as that which preceded
it. An alternative to this somewhat self-defeating line
of reasoning occasionally advanced went like this:
'Why should we tell your generation what we want? If
we do, there is a chance that you will seek to corrupt
our revolutionary purity by proposing a seductive
compromise!'

The popular idols of those who indulged in this
circular dialectic were, of course, Che Guevara, the
Cuban-Argentinian lieutenant of Fidel Castro, who
being dead could not betray the cause by contradicting
any propositions advanced in his name hereinafter, and
Herbert Marcuse, the ex-German political scientist of
San Diego, whose works are almost unreadable and

hence seldom seem to have actually been read by his disciples. Then there were Maoists, with the little red book, and dozens of other schisms and factions too numerous to mention or bother about. The most fanatic of all to emerge thus far was a small but wholly violent group who called themselves the Weathermen, a few score of whom deliberately staged 'four days of rage' in Chicago in the autumn of 1969 during which they smashed up cars, windows and shop fronts in a frenzy of violence, the sole object of which was to provoke 'the pigs' into blazing action with CS gas and night sticks flashing. The police duly obliged.

It seems almost incredible now but as late as 1964 it was fashionable for American educators and liberals generally to deplore the conformist tendencies of the nation's youth. They were insufficiently politicized, the complaint ran. The assassination of John Kennedy had numbed them and LBJ lacked charisma. A sense of cause began to develop with the passage of Johnson's civil rights legislation. A number—never very large— felt impelled to missionary efforts amongst the down-trodden blacks of the Deep South, helping the hitherto disenfranchised to register to vote and taking part in various protest marches—often at considerable physical risk. But it was not until the spring of 1965 that the so-called Free Speech Movement was well and truly launched on the University of California's sprawling campus at Berkeley, San Francisco, by a 22-year-old New Yorker named Mario Savio.

Savio, who had been busy as a civil rights activist in Mississippi, announced that he was 'tired of reading history—I want to make it!' He organized a series of protests, boycotts, sit-ins and the like, not only for free speech, which meant plain foul language for its own sake, but also for banning the bomb, against the Viet-

nam war and denouncing Alabama's Wallace. It cul-
minated in a victory of sorts in forcing the resignation
of the university's president, Clark Kerr. There were
also clashes with police. Politically it produced the
opposite of its intention—a sharp swing to the right in
California with the election of Reagan as law-and-order
Republican Governor.

Earnest analysis of this early unruliness, which in
due course spread eastwards back across America, have
tended to put it all down to the frustrations of the computer age. They saw the student as being increasingly
crushed by the exacting demands of specialization. The
bigger US universities are so vast that it is impossible
for professors to know or even to meet personally more
than a fraction of the boys and girls they teach. It is
not uncommon, for example, for 2,000 students to
attend a lecture in some vast hall while yet more, often
scores of miles away on another campus, are sitting in
on the same performance piped in by closed-circuit
TV. Several State universities boast 30,000 or more
students. The feeling of being little more than an auto-
maton in a network of irrelevant studies controlled by
punch-cards fed to master automata is easily acquired.
Then there are the social and parental pressures on the
American child to 'make the grade'. Since already one-
half of the youngsters who emerge from the secondary
school system are expected to go on to college it flows
inevitably from this that a mere bachelor's degree is
scarcely a passport to a good job. Indeed, the latest
phenomenon is that PhDs are in serious over-supply.
This in turn is making it more important to go to a
prestige college than to win the highest qualifications a
less well-known one can confer.

Students tend to be particularly disaffected in the
Arts and social sciences—the soft disciplines. Not only

do many students doubt whether what they are being taught is worth knowing, but so do some oddly assorted elders. Spiro Agnew, the Vice-President Nixon picked with uncanny skill to function as his political lightning conductor, is one: Gore Vidal, the novelist, is another. Agnew thinks that overemphasis on higher education is denying many a potentially good plumber useful earning time: Vidal thinks it serves as a means of fudging employment statistics—a parking lot in the passage from childhood into life. Educators, needless to say, disagree—and with one another, too.

The problem is compounded if not caused by affluence—the same affluence that permits American middle-class youngsters to indulge their whims in experimenting with marihuana, LSD and other more dangerous hard drugs to the degree that it is now becoming a real menace in secondary schools. Parental control, never a strong point with the beneficiaries of Dr Benjamin Spock's popular pediatric teachings, is minimal. American youngsters often seem actively to despise their mothers and fathers—certainly to a much more evident degree than in, say, Britain. The generation gap is real: not only that, but such wiseacres as Dr Margaret Meade, the anthropologist, who ardently supports the cult of youth-knows-best, testify that it is inevitable and right that it should be so.

It can be argued that the child is right to question whether it is worth so much effort to attend his classes in order to end up in the kind of dead-end job his father holds down. The computer age is palpably reducing a widening range of middle and upper-middle executives in business and government into little more than mechanized clerks. The function of decision-making, which alone distinguished the salaried white-collar worker from lowlier, wage-earning office help, can increasingly be turned over to a data-processor. For example, whereas once upon a time it was up to a local bank branch manager to judge a customer's creditworthiness in respect of a loan for a new car or improvements to his house, nowadays he is not encouraged to do anything more than feed the required information on to a card for the benefit of a centralized memory bank, which makes its ruling in the form of a 'read-out'.

When a dock worker loses his job to a fork-lift it is seldom before his union has succeeded in coming to terms with management. This has been the pattern in getting automation accepted in America much faster than elsewhere. The union agrees to accelerate retirements in return for management's contributing large sums to its pension funds, for example. A bargain is struck. The docker who is duly found redundant has fewer illusions about his place in the scheme of things. He is content to go fishing or start a new career in some other field. But the educated executive, shunted aside by the cybernetic age, is emotionally less able to cope with it. How do you tell a man who has been earning $15,000 a year or more and has his name on the glass door of his cubicle that a thing of plastic tapes, whirling discs and ciphers has effectively displaced him? But his son may interpret the message only too accurately.

The modern American child, too, to an even greater degree than his European counterpart, is apt never to have known a situation where three meals a day failed to materialize. His parents may bore him with reminiscences of the Depression years or the War. He will half heed them, if he heeds them at all. He is, in short, pampered and spoiled, much more indulged than loved. On top of this, he—and his sister—are constantly exposed to the mendacities of high-pressure advertising on the TV and in the Press. They are endlessly regaled with news and comment that reveals politicians as charlatans, crooks, self-seekers—and very many indeed certainly are. They cannot visit the drug store newsstand without being confronted by the assumption that their entire generation (and a good part of the nation) is sex-obsessed or queer, high on pot and copping out. Lawlessness and corruption is condemned by the same elders as condone it—and profit from it. They perceive on all sides abundant evidence that the society they are expected to inherit is a very sick one, whose values and priorities are in a terrifying tangle.

The youngsters, who turned to McCarthy as a kind of Pied Piper in 1968, found in him a safety-valve for their pent-up frustrations. It often struck me watching him that they invented him as a symbol rather than that they followed him. He would have made a very strange President if by some astonishing miracle he had been elected. His philosophy of office was so excessively low key he would have been well nigh invisible. He would frequently remark, for example, on how he felt the White House should be turned into a museum with the fences torn down. Except that he was thoroughly against the Vietnam war, he was dispassionate to the point of vacuum on most issues. He could also be bafflingly recondite before mystified audiences: I once heard him, for example, deliver a fearsomely technical lecture on the problems of international monetary liquidity to a convivial gathering of master builders and their wives in Wisconsin. It can hardly have won him many votes. But the kids, although sometimes in despair at these antics, adored him to a point where it began to worry responsible adults in his party: what on earth was going to happen to them when the adventure ended?

In the eyes of America's well-to-do liberals, the unrest in the nation's schools is largely due to Vietnam. This may be so in *their* schools, perhaps, but in poorer districts it is more due to racial tension and crime. The common denominator in both is an alarming growth in drug addiction amongst the young. I would not suggest that a majority are nowadays 'hooked', but rather that it is fashionable both in the ghetto and in white suburbia to be hip to the drug scene. A quarter-million kids slept out at Woodstock at a mass folk music concert, in their bell-bottoms and beads. They experienced the great universal love-in feeling of cause and solidarity by marching on the Washington monument to protest. All this may sound as harmless as Beatlemania, but American children do not do things by halves. The pot cult became almost conformist. Spot-checks of public and private schools all over the country in 1969 showed that scarcely any were free of this drug problem and one-in-ten was seriously worried about heroin. Senator Tom Dodd stated in Congress in January 1970 that drug addiction had become the principal medical problem in the US armed forces and that, at a conservative estimate, 12 million Americans have taken marihuana and 250,000 are addicted to heroin.

The 'Woodstock nation' was not quite as sweet as it had seemed at first. *Time* magazine reported on the pop festival in August 1969 in ecstatic terms. It 'turned out to be history's largest happening,' the paper recorded, '...the moment when the special culture of US youth of the '60s displayed its strength, appeal and power...may well rank as one of the significant political and sociological events of the age.' In fact, this lionizing of a counter-culture spawned by the flower-people of San Francisco's Haight-Ashbury and cemented by hard rock music and dope was a foolish attempt on the part of the over-30s to participate vicariously in the seemingly enviable freedom of Youth. Americans of the kind that get to be magazine writers and editors are mortally afraid of seeming square. And doubtless this accounts for their failure to record subsequently that Woodstock died five months later at Altamont outside Berkeley, California, when an attempt to repeat the magical Connecticut rally ended hideously. It was estimated afterwards that 500,000 turned out for this second all-day concert, stars of which were Mick Jagger and the Rolling Stones. Someone had engaged the notorious Hells Angels—a gang of motorbike-riding thugs—as guards. This in itself was enough to guarantee tragedy, which came surely enough. Four youngsters were killed. A black boy was ritually stabbed to death by Angels right under Jagger's nose as he sang 'Sympathy for the devil' on stage. Over 100 were beaten up by these same hoodlums with clubs and chains. Perhaps 1,000 were treated for LSD overdoses. At least two performers were hospitalized—one of them a pregnant girl singer. *Time* magazine, having waxed so eloquent about Woodstock earlier, overlooked its Californian sequel which was surely quite as 'significant . . . of the age'.

It is not my purpose to moralize about drugs. Suffice it to say that youngsters who take even the soft drug do so partly because it is socially accepted but more so because it releases tensions—and it is, in turn, this which they have turned into their excuse. The slum-dweller is buying oblivion from his miserable surroundings, and then resorts to robbery with violence to pay the pusher: the better-off suburbanite seeks release from the hang-ups that derive from inner conflicts of a more sophisticated kind. The fact remains that the entire hippie/youth revolt/ghetto riot/crime-in-the-streets/ drug scene is stirring up a powerful groundswell of reaction in Middle America against the young—its own young included.

Dr Calvin Plimpton, head of the excellent, if expensive, New England private school named Amherst, recently wrote an open letter to Nixon ascribing the 'turmoil on the campus' to the failure of political leaders to address themselves 'effectively, massively and persistently (to) the major social and foreign problems of our times'. He was doubtless sincere—and was much quoted in prestige newspapers—when he said the uproar in the universities 'derives from the distance separating the American dream from the American reality'. This is a factor and I have touched on it earlier. But in my view it has been the hypocrisy of teaching the young for so long that the dream and the reality are one that has created much of the problem. Dr Plimpton's Amherst statement had it that 'huge expenditure of national resources for military purposes...the critical needs of America's 30 million poor, the unequal division of our life on racial issues' are responsible for the 'malaise of the larger society'. It is probably much truer that his more idealistic students—one of whom is David Eisenhower, Nixon's son-in-law—find it impossible to square dropping napalm on Vietnamese villagers in order to save them from Communism as part of an imperial mission with the anti-colonialist tradition he has been led to believe is his heritage. A less inhibited and probably larger group is just as badly disturbed over the failure of American armed might to produce instant results.

Here, then, one comes to the other ugly factor emerging in American politics. Nixon was more haunted in 1968 by Wallace than by Humphrey. George Wallace took 13·5 per cent of the popular vote nationwide and won the five solidly segregationist States of the old South where the American Civil War lives on. There can be no greater mistake than to ignore the phenomenon of his support in the North also. Wallace goes down very well amongst the natural enemies of the better-off, better-educated McCarthy kids—who are to be found amongst the other half of the secondary school output that does not get to go to university. The poor whites of the South and the blue-collar workers who live in big city suburbs in the industrial regions of the Middle West, for example, feel threatened by the advances the American Negro made under Johnson. They know that blacks moving into the house next door as a result of anti-discrimination laws knocks down the value of their mortgaged homes. Tell them that this will only be temporary and that in due time the problem will iron itself out and you are not apt to get their votes. They also know that the forced integration of State schools depresses educational standards even if this should not be so in theory. It is easy to be liberal, they argue bitterly, in a lily-white suburb or if one is rich enough to send one's youngsters to fee-paying institutions.

Nixon may still be haunted by this Wallace spectre. If anything should complicate Nixon's plan to disengage from the war, he will be in deep trouble—and so will America: a country divided against itself, full of doubts and fears and looking inwards. The tide may well be turning away from acceptance of the policy recommendations of an educated élite—and against the élite. The day of the simplistic know-nothing yahoo may be dawning.

I I

Black and White

The problem of race is certainly the most intractable of all that the United States faces. It is also the most damaging. It could well prove to be more serious than any threats from the Russians, Chinese, or even of an economic slump. Its very existence naggingly and everlastingly questions the American ideal enshrined in the Declaration of Independence: 'We hold these Truths to be selfevident, that all Men are created equal...'

The plain fact is that Americans of black African ancestry are not the equals, even today, of their white fellow countrymen. Although over a century has passed since Abraham Lincoln wrote the Emancipation Proclamation that freed the slaves, and despite five major Civil Rights bills having been enacted by the Congress since 1957, discrimination against the Negro minority, which constitutes eleven per cent of the nation's population, continues.

Colour bars exist in countries other than the US—including black ones—but the important difference is that there is less hypocrisy about it elsewhere. As Gunnar Myrdal pointed out in *The American Dilemma* 'Americans of all national origins, classes, regions, creeds, and colours have something in common: a set of beliefs, a political creed. This American Creed is the cement in the diversified structure of this great nation.' The Negro in America also believes in the creed but knows it is not lived up to: the white majority knows it too. This fact sets up strains of a peculiarly schizo-phrenic kind.

The melting pot theory favoured during the turn of the century days of massive immigration from Europe, assumed that ultimately a new all-American man would be bred out of the many races—given plenty of time, of course, and no undue shoving. The existence of a minority which does not respond is a continual affront to the creed. Yet the Negroes were in America long before the Irish, the Italians, the Greeks and Poles and the rest. They were also in the country involuntarily, having been sold into slavery by fellow Africans and shipped in monstrously barbarous fashion to the New World by Anglo-Saxon sea captains.

Slavery existed elsewhere in the Americas, to be sure. But it has to be recognized that there was a peculiarly inhuman quality to the institution as practised in the largely Protestant north compared with that obtaining where the more relaxed traditions of Mediterranean Roman Catholicism held sway. The Spaniards and Portu-guese colonists in Latin America may have butchered the Indians, Aztecs and Caribs, but they did not tear husband from wife, mother from child, and buy and sell people like cattle the way the North Americans did. The English settlers and plantation owners regarded their slaves as chattels and would not permit them to learn to read or write. They were frequently not even allowed to marry—merely to breed slaves for their owner to sell.

There are few pure-bred black Negroes in America today. The notion that miscegenation is an offence against nature and a major sin may have been widely held but it was also certainly very substantially in-dulged in. This in turn explains yet another aspect of the guilt complex that sensitive Americans have about the race question and especially the sexual taboos that surround it. It also is what makes the race problem in America so different in quality from that which has recently been developing in Britain, for example. The American Negro is no immigrant who, if he dislikes the New World, can return to his native land. He was raised in his native land for more than three centuries. Yet only in the '60s, and then more legally than actually, has he achieved the same rights as the most recent recipient of US citizenship papers.

Slavery was not the basic issue of the American Civil War, of course. What was contested was the right of the Southern States to secede from the Union. Lincoln's emancipation proclamation in 1863 was intended to hurt the Southerners' plantation economy rather than to undo a wrong. When the war ended, the South was, indeed, ruined anyway and it has remained a relative backwater ever since, relying on injections of northern capital and Federal aid funds to make such halting progress as it has. Nonetheless, in popular American mythology the war was about slavery and the air of virtuousness that Northerners display towards Southerners on the subject is a continuing and deep irritation, corroding national unity.

A cause of great bitterness in the South, which lingers on, was the way in which during the immediate post-Civil War days Northern carpet-baggers descended like locusts in pursuit of concessions of one kind and another in the South, installing easily corrupted, newly freed black slaves in State legislatures as willing tools in a systematic extortion of the vanquished. Gradually the Southerners recovered enough to whittle down the rights of the blacks. The cynicism of the North was then evident in that Washington made no attempt to uphold them. White supremacy was reintroduced by means of lynchings and terrorism, followed by the reimposition of a serfdom that in many ways was worse than slavery. The Negro was deprived of his vote: 'Jim Crow' segregation laws were imposed on him. He paid dearly for his short-lived emancipation.

Over the years and at an ever-increasing rate, black Americans have migrated northwards and to the Far West because of economic pressures. From being largely rural, America's Negro population is now mainly urban. In the past 30 years since the beginning of the Second World War, the proportion of blacks living in the South has dropped from 77 per cent to 52 per cent. At the same time, they have been gradually taking over the major metropolitan areas themselves. As whites have migrated towards the suburbs, so Negroes have consolidated in the cities to the extent that by 1969 some 55 per cent of all America's blacks were central city dwellers—which meant, in plain language, they lived in the slums.

The population of the District of Columbia—that is, of Washington proper—was at least 70 per cent black in 1970. In 1950, according to census figures, it was 35 per cent. This surge is the real reason why the District is the only one of its size in America to have no elected local government of its own. It has instead a Presidentially appointed 'mayor', who is black, named Walter Washington. But the final say in how the capital of the leading nation of the free world is run is tenaciously clung to by the District Committee of Congress—a body in which illiberal diehard white Southerners hold sway. They have effectively withheld the municipal franchise from Washington's largely black population. It is ironic that a capital which for years was highly critical of the colonial exploitation once supposedly practised by the British, French and others, should itself be subject to colonial rule to this day. The powers-that-be reckon that Washingtonians are 'not ready yet for the vote!'

As recently as 1964, segregation was enforced in the South in public parks, in buses, at drug store lunch counters and in hotels, motels and restaurants, cinemas and lavatories. Negroes were also discriminated against by being kept off the electoral rolls by such devices as loaded literacy tests—impossibly difficult tests being put to blacks and perfunctory ones to whites. Yet most Southern whites quite sincerely believed—and still do— that those were happier times when the 'nigrah' knew his place.

It was subtler in the North. But even after it was declared unconstitutional, the system continued of denying Negroes the right to buy houses in certain areas of cities or suburbs by requiring white purchasers to enter into covenants binding themselves never to sell to a coloured person. In several of Washington's city and country clubs it was—and in some still is as late as 1970—against the rules for members to have a Negro guest on the premises. Not long ago a prospective member of the famous Chevy Chase Club was turned down on the grounds that he had allegedly once entertained Ralph Bunche, the Negro Nobel prizewinner and top United Nations official, in his home. As it happened, he had never met Dr Bunche in his life.

It has been common practice in the South, since the enactment of the Civil Rights' bills of the '60s, to restrict to white use formerly public golf courses, for example, by converting them into private clubs. This is, of course, a deliberate twisting of the law and it is, therefore, improper for a law officer to connive at such moves. But when it was pointed out to Nixon that a Southern judge, whom he had named for the US Supreme Court, the highest bench in the land, had been guilty of such conspiracy, he replied: 'If everybody in government service who has belonged or does belong to restricted golf clubs were to leave the service, this city would have the highest rate of unemployment of any city in the country.' That remark was made at the White House in Washington on January 30, 1970. Shortly afterwards, the National Association for the Advancement of Coloured People, which is definitely a moderate body, accused the Nixon Administration of abandoning the national goal of an integrated society. It complained that pressures in support of segregation are great and if not opposed (they) will destroy the hope that this can be one nation. Senator Edward Brooke, a Republican but the only Negro in the Senate, bitterly attacked his own party chiefs for wooing Southern whites at the expense of blacks like himself, who want to share the American Dream.

Evidence of how pressure was exercised within the White House was soon revealed after Harry Dent, a former aide to Senator Strom Thurmond of South Carolina, became a liaison officer to Nixon. It was, after all, Thurmond who swung the crucial Southern votes to Nixon in 1968 that secured him the Presidency—votes that might otherwise have gone to Alabama's George Wallace. Once installed as Thurmond's man in the Executive Office, Dent went to work pulling strings to block the implementation of Federal desegregation rulings in such a way as to help the Republicans consolidate. He dug up wealthy Southerners who would pay lavish contributions to Party funds in return for a slowing down of schools' integration. And when in 1970 this was disclosed in the Press, he did not trouble to deny it.

As Dent saw it, Nixon had made a campaign pledge to ease up on the South—the white South, that is—and he would suffer if he failed to make good on it. The chance to construct a secure national majority that could be relied on to return the Californian to the White House in 1972 for a second term would be thrown away.

In the circumstances that pertain in America today it is hardly surprising that the Negro community feels cheated. What is amazing is how belatedly the nation's white liberals came to realize that the time had arrived to take concrete steps to end discrimination. Roosevelt did little about it. It was not until Truman was in office that segregation was ended within the US armed forces. The Supreme Court of the United States ruled in 1954 in favour of schools' desegregation for the first time, although it took 10,000 troops to restore order in Little Rock, Arkansas three years later when the first nine black children were put in a white school there. In 1962 two people, including a French journalist, were killed at Oxford, Mississippi, in a riot occasioned by the forced admission of a single Negro, James Meredith, to the State university there. And in 1963, Medgar Evers, a Negro leader in Jackson, Mississippi, was shot by a man who has never been punished to this day.

Americans have a peculiar blind spot on the race issue. It is a matter of record that the late Robert Kennedy only finally saw the light on the subject as result of a curious encounter arranged for him in the early summer of 1963, just weeks before Evers was murdered. He was his brother's Attorney-General at the time when, at last, it seems to have dawned on Camelot that a black-white crisis of unsuspected seriousness was developing and the moment was ripe for what was referred to as 'a second emancipation declaration'—the first having been Lincoln's of a century earlier.

What spurred this was not so much the then recent race riots in Birmingham, Alabama, as a personal meeting between the younger Kennedy and a group of a dozen Negro personalities, none of them previously prominent politically, whom he had asked to an informal chat at his father's luxurious flat off New York's Central Park.

The session, which lasted three painful hours, was an eye-opener for all involved. It revealed the depths of the chasm that separated the minds of America's best-intentioned Establishment liberals and the black minority. The guests included Harry Belafonte, the Jamaican actor; Lena Horne, the nightclub star; James Baldwin, the novelist; Lorraine Hansbury, the playwright (*A Raisin in the Sun*); Jerome Smith, a 25-year-old veteran of the famous 'Freedom Rides' to break down the Jim Crow system in the South's public transportation system, and Dr Kenneth Clark, a Harlem psychologist.

All the participants, who were handpicked by Baldwin at Kennedy's personal request, had achieved success in the white man's world, save only Jerry Smith. As Dr Clark afterwards told me: 'It developed swiftly from dialogue to diatribe.' But he did not think it had been a pointless encounter. 'There was communication,' he explained. 'We all saw that afterwards. The fact that the Kennedys saw the need and that the meeting took place at all and lasted as long as it did was a distinct plus—the more so in that it brought home to us how badly needed such exchanges were. For the first time, I do think the Attorney-General, as he was at the time, heard how the Negro people—and not just recognized leaders like Dr Martin Luther King—could no longer be asked to be "reasonable".'

Robert Kennedy had flown in from Washington for the talk, which was to lead to others, accompanied by his special assistant, Burke Marshall, who had represented him in the Birmingham troubles earlier—those were the riots in which police turned dogs loose on black demonstrators, it may be recalled, pictures of which shocked the world.

Dr Clark said that what rattled Kennedy from the outset was a flat statement by Jerry Smith to the effect that he found it 'nauseous' that there had to be any such discussion. He added that he and others in his age group felt no sense of identity with their white-co-nationals. Specifically, he insisted that they would not 'follow the flag' if called upon to help liberate Cuba from Communism. (This was, of course, before Vietnam arose to haunt America.) 'This shocked Kennedy no end,' said Dr Clark. 'He never quite recovered. But for our part, we were shocked that he was shocked and that he seemed genuinely unable to understand Jerry's argument. It showed a strange *naïveté....*'

Attempts to repair the damage were unavailing. But Baldwin spoke for the rest, Clark went on, when he declared that 'Jerry Smith was the most important person in the room'. In vain, Kennedy sought to make a case for proceeding step by step towards Negro emancipation. His guests stolidly replied that the time for 'deals' had ended. 'We told him that a fundamental moral issue had arisen affecting America's posture as the leader of the democratic world and that it was time —high time—for his brother, the President, to show greatness and not wriggle and manoeuvre.'

At this point, Jerry Smith said that the next time a Negro youth sought admission to a Southern all-white university, the President of the United States should personally conduct him thither instead of calling out the troops. 'This obviously stunned Bobby—he couldn't see it our way,' Clark recalled. 'But the fact that he wanted to talk at all showed he was not a devil. There were no devils that afternoon—only an ugly past that was still very much with us.'

The Harlem psychologist was obviously much moved by the entire experience at the time. His son, whom I met shortly afterwards, was far less impressed. 'Just a bunch of actors and actresses,' was his comment. 'It's too late for that. We want our place in the sun and we aren't waiting for the whites to give it to us.'

Nonetheless, the American black was already making strenuous advances. In the early days of the Civil Rights' movement of the 1960s, there was considerable fraternal feeling between young whites and blacks. The former, as college students on vacation, would brave the wrath of the Dixie rednecks—'poor white trash'—to make the pilgrimage into the South to help blacks get on the electoral rolls, for example. They felt uplifted by the experience and the not inconsiderable personal dangers involved. Some got murdered in the process— like the two young New Yorkers who, with a Negro friend, were callously killed by Ku Klux Klansmen at Philadelphia, Mississippi, with the blatant complicity of the local law officers. Others were savagely beaten up. Their assailants were seldom, if ever, caught or convicted.

It fell to Lyndon Johnson, first as Vice-President and then, after Kennedy's assassination, as President, to push through the Civil Rights and Voting Rights Acts that were at last to secure the Negro the equality under the law that any non-American might well have imagined had been his for a hundred years by virtue of the US Constitution. For a while there was a brief euphoria. But it soon became tragically evident that racial hatreds built up over generations were not about to be swept aside by legislation, however well-meaning. Desegregation has been consistently resisted by Southern whites who have, not without reason, accused their

Northern fellow countrymen of hypocrisy on the subject, particularly in connection with State schools. On the black side, the pent up fury of centuries was readily exploited, together with the bitterness which derived from the cruel discovery that laws do not change men's hearts.

Inevitably the main collision has been between poor whites and blacks rather than the well-to-do. Nowhere is discrimination practised more effectively than in certain key Trades Unions. It has not helped matters, that, in order to demonstrate their enlightenment, many big companies have made a practice of hiring showpiece blacks to put in their front offices. The same thing happens in the better universities and private schools, which like to be generous with scholarships for token Negroes to an extent where whites have begun to feel overcompensated against.

Meanwhile the love affair between youthful white Northern liberals and southern blacks had soon cooled. The former began to find a more exciting cause in opposition to the Vietnam war and the latter became increasingly attracted to the slogan 'Black Power', first launched by the Student Nonviolent Co-ordinating Committee (Snick) under the Trinidadian, Stokeley Carmichael, and Rap Brown, when that movement purged itself of its white membership in 1965. Already coming into prominence at that stage were Negro leaders who did not want integration. The Black Muslim movement headed by a strangely pale fanatic who styles himself Elijah Muhammad was gaining strength in America's big city slums. He had seized on Islam simply to symbolize antagonism to the white man's Christianity rather than because he was taken with the religion itself. It was a powerful way of making his point. The Churches have greatly influenced the Negro but they have also kept him docile. The Black Muslims preach that this is how the white devil has conspired to keep the coloured races enslaved.

Malcolm X, a sometime pimp and drug runner, who reformed under Muslim influence, was later to break with Muhammad when he discovered true Islam as result of a pilgrimage to Mecca. He then learnt that there are areas of the world where colour is not as obsessive a subject as it is in America. He began to see that there might be some redeeming features about light-skinned persons. He was about to venture off into fascinating new heresies when he was assassinated by black gunmen. He has now joined the pantheon of those heroes of the Western world's radicals, militants and fuzzily confused, like Che Guevara, Ho Chi Minh and Frantz Fanon. Malcolm's death has kept this image pure. He is one slum black who really frightened whitey. And now increasingly any Negro leader who would do less can hardly hope to be popular with his community's young.

The Black Muslims, as such, have been superseded by other groups. They were possibly too ascetic to attract a mass following. But the style they set is a far more important thing than is their sect itself. It is a style which says black is beautiful, and to aspire to join the white man's world is to commit soul suicide. Theirs is the doctrine that offers a way out of the frustration of chasing a will o' the wisp: the dream of one America.

As a successful black magazine writer Simeon Booker, put it to me: 'We are moving towards a situation where the ugly division is not so much between black and white as between white nigger and black nigger. The white nigger is the one who still thinks and hopes he can get the whites to accept him. He likes all the same things—the cars and colour television, nice clothes and fancy vacations and all that stuff. He keeps getting hurt but he's a glutton for punishment. Then there's the poor black nigger who just isn't ever going to make it even that far because he just hasn't the job training or anything. He'll just rot. But now there's the black nigger coming up who can make it in the white world, maybe better than the white nigger, but he wants no part of it. He's smart and he's tough. But if there's a thing he hates more than whitey, it's that white nigger.'

By the time of his death, in 1968, Dr Martin Luther King, the Nobel prize-winner, was already a falling star. He could still stir the hearts of blacks and whites. Five years earlier when he preached to the biggest inter-racial ingathering ever staged in Washington from the steps of the Lincoln Memorial. 'I have a dream...' he said. It was a nation where black and white would live together in sweet harmony. Hours before he was assassinated he was asserting in a sermon. 'I have been to the mountain top...I have seen the promised land....' He died still hopeful. But a much more bitter realism was already rapidly permeating the rising generation.

The nationwide riots that followed Dr King's assassination, including the burning down of several downtown blocks of Washington itself, were a spectacular tribute to his memory. The damage was fantastic from arson and looting. And it was at last, and reluctantly, realized that no genuine progress had been made towards harmonizing race relations. They had merely been polarized more completely than ever.

With admirable candour, the report of a special investigation into the causes of recent race riots headed by Illinois' Governor Kerner informed President Johnson flatly: 'Our nation is moving towards two societies: one black, one white, separate and unequal.' It squarely blamed what it termed 'white racism' for this state of affairs, which was naturally resented, even if true. But since then black racism has become quite as strong.

Ever since the long, hot summers of 1967 and 1968, both blacks and whites have been arming themselves in fear of each other. In the particularly riot-prone city of Newark, New Jersey, it has reached the point where white and black extremists have found it convenient to install a 'hot line' over which they can communicate in case some minor incident threatens to flare into a major conflict. Hostilities have thus been formalized and an armed truce established on the basis of an altogether credible balance of deterrents.

The white liberals working to better the lot of the blacks have characteristically been largely confined to the better-off and better-educated, whose affluence permits them to live in securely white enclaves and send their children to private schools. This has tended to introduce an element of class conflict into the equation, further compounding the bitterness of middle- and lower-income whites against the Establishment—just as Vietnam has done. This explains why an outright and unabashed segregationist like Alabama's former Governor, George Wallace, is not only strongly supported by Southern whites but by working-class Northerners as well. As these people see it, their intellectual superiors who have so long dominated the Federal Government not only want to force their children into schools with blacks, and give blacks their jobs but also conscript their sons for a war of their own making. To add insult to injury, the sons of these well-to-do are not only the loudest critics of that war but are also in the best position to avoid being conscripted for it by securing educational deferments, bribing doctors to declare them medically unfit or simply flitting the country.

A nightmare situation has thus emerged where blacks

hate whites and whites hate blacks and both despise the liberal political leaders, educators and social engineers whose attempts to cure ancient wrongs have gone so horribly awry. On the theory that racial equality should begin in the schools, it was not enough to desegregate them. Reform-minded authorities began insisting on transporting children in buses across cities to achieve a balanced black-white mix in the classrooms. Parents objected—sometimes violently. In some instances the system was patently absurd—in Washington, where 93 per cent of the youngsters attending State schools are black, children were bussed miles from their homes in an effort to achieve a mix that was obviously unattainable.

Instead of improving race relations, the tensions rapidly transferred themselves to the schoolyard. State secondary schools swiftly became the newest area of racial violence not only between blacks and whites, but in many instances of black militants ganging up with teenage white radicals against their teachers and school heads. There were no fewer than 900 arrests in northern State high schools in the first *two months* of the 1970 scholastic year, for various crimes, including murder and arson. The casualty list in that brief period included 200 injured, of which 20 were policemen and 12 teachers. In Washington it was found necessary to recruit special police guards to stem classroom violence which had gone far beyond the ability of underpaid teachers to control. The practice was common in other cities as well. In short, the entire educational process began to degenerate into bedlam in an alarmingly high proportion of the nation's schools.

The full impact of this fantastic state of affairs will only be felt in a few years' time. The breakdown in secondary education can hardly fail to affect standards in universities later on, where turmoil has become virtually an accepted feature of academic life. The notion that campus violence has become a thing of the past as a result of the Nixon policy of disengaging US troops as fast as possible from Vietnam is unhappily baseless. It is undoubtedly true that a majority of America's undergraduates would prefer to get on with their studies—but that always was the case. It is also true that the focus of dissent is liable to change: New causes will be found. But violence, as a Negro militant observed tartly recently, 'is as American as Mom's cherry pie!'

In the context of race, violence has meant an accelerated trend towards effective apartheid as the whites emigrate to the suburbs and surrender the central cities to the blacks. Whereas once upon a time whites would visit black quarters, such as Harlem in New York, and only feel mildly daring, this is seriously no longer recommended. Even in broad daylight there are sections of Washington that are unsafe for whites. The feeling in the Negro community is that the Republicans have put the clock back. The hardening of hearts is mutual. The blacks will admit there have been improvements in that they can now expect to get a table at almost any restaurant or a room in any hotel, and that good jobs are easier to obtain for qualified Negroes than they used to be. But social integration has not advanced. If anything, it has declined. The fashionable hostess no longer feels impelled to cultivate token blacks to grace her dinner table.

Nixon's domestic political strategy requires that he strengthen his support in the South amongst conservatives who formerly were loyal Democrats. He does not need to curry favour with the blacks for this. Moreover, as a matter of broad policy it has been urged on the

President by his chief adviser on urban affairs, Daniel Moynihan, that the moment has come to apply the doctrine of 'benign neglect' to the race issue.

This phrase derives from a remark by the Earl of Durham in the last century about Canada. He argued that Whitehall's benign neglect of the Canadians and their problems had been beneficial in that it had encouraged them to order their own affairs in a manner that suited them to the point that they were perfectly capable of assuming full responsibility for their own government.

Moynihan, who regretted that his confidential memorandum to Nixon had leaked, argued that the American Negro 'is making extraordinary progress' although 'there would seem to be counter-currents that pose a serious threat to the welfare of the blacks and the stability of the society, black and white'. He felt that this was not being cured by too much concentration on the race issue. It had been 'too much talked about' and the 'forum has been taken over by hysterics, paranoids and boodlers on all sides'. He blamed both white and black extremists for this. He suggested that over-zealous police action against the militant Black Panthers, for example, might well have provided them with 'opportunities for martyrdom, heroics, histrionics or whatever'.

The Moynihan approach would be to encourage what he called the 'silent black majority' which 'shares most of the concerns of its white counterpart but is ignored by the government'. There were some signs that this thinking appealed to Nixon. But it also remained a fact that Moynihan had already offended the blacks several years ago in a report he did on the structure of the Negro family which depicted it as a matriarchy in danger of internal collapse.

Predictably, the Irish sociologist's recommendations infuriated white segregationists nearly as much as they did black moderates who were only too well aware that in today's climate they risk being branded 'Uncle Toms' within their community. At a time when Nixon is thought to be using his Vice-President Spiro Agnew to outbid the odious Wallace, the black 'silent majority' Moynihan referred to is in a very exposed position.

Dr Ralph Abernathy, who succeeded Dr King as leader of the Southern Christian Leadership, is no firebrand but he has found it necessary to take the position that the killing of Fred Hampton, a Chicago Black Panther, in a police raid in December 1969, was 'part of a calculated design of genocide'. Genocide is a strong word. To suggest that the Nixon administration, the Federal Bureau of Investigation and the police in various American cities were trying to wipe out the nation's blacks by engaging in gun battles with self-styled marxist-leninist revolutionaries seemed a trifle exaggerated. But Dr Abernathy was not alone in making the charge.

There are probably no more than a few hundred Black Panthers in the entire country. It is also likely that they will, in due course, be superseded by some other armed group, also sporting paramilitary uniforms and striking attitudes of open belligerency against the white 'exploiters', police 'pigs' and the whole apparatus of 'ameriKKKa', as they put it. They are taken seriously by J. Edgar Hoover, the ageing director of the FBI. And in the meantime, they have become folk heroes amongst the black ghetto young. Their great appeal, of course, lies in the contention that the black is not simply as good as the white, but very much better, nobler and braver. They symbolize black *machismo*.

That the Panthers should scare the daylights out of

Middle America while intriguing not a few youthful dissenters, whites included, is not surprising. What is surely stranger is how an organization called the National Black Economic Development Council, headed by a 41-year-old black militant, James Forman, has contrived to raise a very considerable sum of money from white churches by issuing a Black Manifesto demanding $500 million as 'reparation...due to us as people who have been exploited and degraded, brutalized, killed and persecuted'. Forman's Manifesto was issued in April 1969 at a black power conference in Detroit. Many church groups—particularly episcopalians have actually paid 'assessments' levied on them, although not without arousing considerable controversy. It has had no noticeable effect in mollifying the beneficiaries, however.

According to Forman, the blacks of America are destined to be the 'vanguard force' that is to 'liberate all the people in the US and ... coloured people the world around'. Because the blacks are the 'most oppressed (it) follows from the laws of revolution that they must ... assume the leadership, total control and exercise the humanity which is inherent in us.' The black people, he went on, 'must move to protect their black interest by assuming leadership inside the US of everything that exists. The time has passed when we are second in command and the white boy stands on top....

'Racism in the US is so pervasive in the mentality of the whites that only an armed, well-disciplined, black-controlled government can ensure the stamping out of racism in this country,' he said flatly. It was in these terms that he justified 'the revolutionary right' of America's blacks to demand the sum in reparations from 'white christian churches and jewish synagogues which are part and parcel of the system of capitalism'.

Forman says the money will be spent on creating a southern land bank to enable black farmers to set up co-operatives, to open radio and television stations, movie studios and publishing houses, set up a black university and to fund the establishment of businesses 'in our motherland Africa'. While it remains somewhat doubtful whether his target figure will ever be achieved, several hundred thousand dollars have thus far rolled in from guilt-ridden churchgoers. This alone surely testifies to the uniqueness of America's race relations problem. Slaves have been freed before but it is hard to recall any previous instance of their descendants being subsidized by those of their former masters to take over control of the State.

It could be argued that this strange affair of reparations is indicative of a deeply Christian spirit, a higher morality that will pave the way to racial harmony in America. No doubt this is the pious hope of the donors. I personally consider it more in the nature of *Danegelt*. It is in any case sadly typical of the American character to think that you can buy your way out of absolutely anything—with money. Yet here is a problem that plainly does not respond to this treatment. Nor can it apparently be solved by any other means. If it could be forgotten, it would be, but it is now—and forever—too obtrusive. The prospect American society must accept is of a substantial alienated minority in its midst. This is why the race issue contributes so greatly to the defeatism that is overtaking thinking Americans.

12

Power and Corruption

'Along with most Americans,' the late Ben Hecht once observed, 'I share the happy gift of forgetfulness. Along with most honest citizens I accept the fact that a goodly percentage of the official administrators and protectors of my American freedom are crooks on the take.'

There is little doubt that his view still prevails. One encounters it constantly even amongst the most passionately patriotic of his countrymen. It really does not seem to disturb the mass of Americans that organized crime—supposedly dominated by a Sicilian Mafia although they are probably credited with more than their share—is big business. Its annual turnover is said to be twice as large as that of General Motors—a statistic which is impossible to verify but is quoted by Justice Department officials from time to time almost with relish.

What bothers Americans far more is not Big Time crime, which is somehow on the verge of being respectable, but petty thievery, armed robbery, rape and violence in the streets. This is another matter: it has made 'law-'n-order' a gut political issue in the nation today. It is an issue, moreover, that quickly assumes a racialist tinge since the incidence of such crime is higher amongst urban blacks—and against fellow blacks, incidentally—than whites who have fled to suburbia.

Since it is no longer safe to wander the streets of any major American city alone after dark, it is scarcely surprising that 'law-'n-order' makes a fine electioneering slogan. In practice, it can be translated into a desire to see law for us and order for them—the conformist majority cracking down on the minority. It does not mean that in the Middle America, where the issue is liveliest, anyone is expecting or even looking for police reform.

Americans by and large do not respect cops. They are not instinctively a law-abiding people the way the British, the Germans, Dutch, Scandinavians and the Japanese tend to be. They even take a peculiar pride in being sturdily independent of the law, preferring self-reliance to the point of anarchy, at least as a theory. This is often put down to the frontier tradition—an amiable conceit in today's standardized, post-industrial era—but has more to do with selfishness and incontinence.

One is often told that Americans substitute the puritan ethic for respect for the law. It is suggested that they resist restraints and controls as a form of 'creeping socialism'. This is invoked particularly as an argument against public welfare projects, State medical services, unemployment insurance and the like. I have encountered ultra conservatives in America who hold that the State is, of itself, an intolerable imposition with its rules and regulations and that to rebel against them is not only normal but basically proper. This extremely romantic view is not one that can readily be put into practice, but it explains something about the affluent American's view of the police as a necessary evil at best and as an adversary at worst.

In some parts of the country the police are indeed not easy to respect in any way. They do not give a fig for the law, as such, for the simple reason that they *are* the law. I had my eyes opened to this in Philadelphia,

Mississippi, in the summer of 1964 when I was assigned to cover the story of the disappearance of three young men—two New Yorkers and a Negro—who had been seized from their car by sheriff's deputies and never seen again alive. The trio had been civil rights' activists engaged in the then-current voter registration drive to get blacks on the local electoral rolls. President Johnson had ordered the FBI to investigate and also called out Federal military forces to search the steaming swampy forests for the missing men.

It rapidly emerged that the local law men were not exactly co-operating with the US Government in this case for the understandable reason that they not only knew that the trio were dead, but also where their bodies were, having been party to killing them. It took six years of intermittent trials to secure conviction of those responsible and even then the crime with which they were charged was not murder but that of having deprived their victims of their civil rights—by taking their lives. It is virtually unknown for a Mississippi jury to convict a white man for killing a black to this day.

The local citizenry could not have been more pleasant to me as a visiting foreigner. They were much less hospitable, however, to their fellow countrymen from the North—the Civil War of over a century ago is still very much alive in those parts. But they were not very reticent. I was told where the bodies would eventually be found by a local journalist over a month before the military unearthed them. It was common knowledge amongst the natives but it was not, apparently, passed on to the FBI since they represented Washington and, therefore, the enemy. I collected from the sheriff's office a recruiting leaflet for the Ku Klux Klan, the hooded white supremacists whose fanatic zeal in pursuit of their cause inclines them to such activities as burning Negro churches and setting fiery crosses in the driveways of backsliding 'nigra-lovers'. The KKK was at that time already branded a terrorist organization by the FBI—in other words, it was officially 'subversive', yet Philadelphia's sheriff and his men were not only members but were inviting 'sober, intelligent, courageous, Christian, white men' to join them because 'the administration of our National Government is now under the actual control of atheists, who are Bolsheviks by nature ... dedicated agents of Satan'.

One could argue that Mississippi is not exactly typical of the United States. But lately its attitudes have been seeping into the lower middle-class or blue-collar North more and more. These attitudes reflect a growing sense of alienation from the Establishment as represented in Washington and also a contempt for its laws not only on the part of citizens but the law men themselves. And this is dangerous: a cancer that feeds on itself.

Corruption—like violence—is also as American as Mom's cherry pie. It comes in many guises. It is not merely a matter of bribery involving petty officials—or of Lyndon Johnson once winning an election by a majority of 87 after a number of long dead Mexican-Americans had voted for him, or even of the stuffed ballot-boxes in Chicago's Cook County securing the State of Illinois for John Kennedy in 1960. It is something deeper. At root it stems from popular toleration, if not actual approval, of Ben Hecht's proposition that many public officials are 'on the take'. It is regarded as the natural order. 'What else does one go into politics for?' 'Politics is a dirty business.' 'Politicians can be bought and sold like anyone else.' It is accepted that mostly 'they are in it for what they can get out of it. Only hypocrites pretend otherwise.' And so on. Visitors to the United States ever since de Tocqueville have been constantly told these things. The sad truth is that there is such abundant evidence to show that they are not entirely an exaggeration.

It is often observed today that America's courts are so overloaded with work, and the law is so weighted in favour of the criminal, that a gunman who is caught robbing a bank will often be out on bail, with the chance to commit a second and third such crime, before he has been punished for the original offence. The chances of a thief's getting away with a single stick-up are about 20 to 1. In short, crime does pay. But while this is statistically proven, there is strikingly little fuss made about peculation of one kind and another at a much higher level.

This is what is upsetting America's youthful idealists as much as the Vietnam war or pollution of the environment. They are in a minority, to be sure, and they do not know what they want as clearly as what they do not. Many—the vast majority—will no doubt settle down to the rat race as their parents did, being unable to articulate their frustrations; but with the spread of awareness through education and the vast acceleration of communications the restive minority is bound to become more and more querulous.

The question that arises is whether the American system which places such incredible executive power in the hands of a single individual combining the functions of elected monarch and his own Prime Minister is capable of the self-cleansing that is needed. George Reedy, who was Johnson's first Press secretary, believes the weakness of the White House is that the incumbent is swiftly surrounded by lackeys who insulate him from political reality by a wall of flattery. It becomes impossible for the President to remain aware of what is really going on : neither he nor the system that supports him is open to the normal scrutiny to which, for example, a British Prime Minister and his cabinet ministers are subjected to daily in the House of Commons at Question Time. On the side of the judiciary, the Supreme Court is not responsive to the increasingly complicated demands of a fast-changing domestic situation. The Constitution of the Founding Fathers, with its famous checks and balances, was not devised to govern so complex, disparate, restless and unhappy a society of 200 million as is the US today.

To put their house in order Americans will first have to cure themselves of accepting, with Ben Hecht, the leadership of 'crooks on the take'. It is no use calling for 'law-'n-order' in a country where it is common knowledge, for example, that a high Congressional official can be exposed and convicted for corrupt practice, tax evasion and flagrant abuse of a position of trust and (for years to go by) without his having paid a fine or served a day in prison. A United States Senator mixes up his political campaign funds with his own money, accepts free hotel suites from companies evidently seeking favours of him, is reprimanded mildly by his peers after being exposed, and again becomes liable to tax fraud proceedings—and gets away with it. Nobody minds: it has happened before and will happen again. After all, there are literally hundreds of lobbyists representing every sort of interest, industry and profession in Washington, whose purpose in life is to persuade Congressmen to vote this way or that. They entertain lavishly and are generous with contributions towards election expenses. These men earn their keep. Many of them are highly respected lawyers whose principal stock-in-trade is their influence in Government. Every now and again the question is raised as to what, precisely, they do for their clients. This can have comic results as in the case where a very well-known White House-level consultant admitted that his firm had received a substantial fee from a major industrialist but denied he had ever done anything to earn it—whereupon the income tax authorities disallowed the industrialist's claim that said fee was a legitimate and therefore a deductible business expense.

Americans who think it odd that a certain southern Senator, James Eastland, should enjoy a farm subsidy of $146,792 in 1969 to compensate him for the cotton he did not grow are apt to be dismissed as radical troublemakers. Eastland is a member of the Agricultural Committee and chairman of the Judiciary Committee. For years the Federal Government has failed to rescind farm subsidy regulations, originally intended to protect the 'little man' from the consequences of overproduction, which allow for such anomalous subsidies as that I have quoted. Few people blame Eastland for getting what he can.

It is perhaps unfair to single out individual legislators for obloquy in this regard. It is not altogether their fault that this is the way the system operates. Political spoils are part of the game and the game is not always and inevitably played for personal profit. For example, influential members of the Armed Services Committee may indeed see that some new and expensive weapon, aircraft or ship, say, can very well be manufactured in their constituencies thus rewarding faithful voters and contributing to the nation's security at the same time. And in its turn, the Pentagon itself is the biggest lobbyist of them all spending millions of dollars a year of the American taxpayers' money on its special task force of Congressional liaison officers to educate Senators and House Representatives on Services' needs. A recent count disclosed that the Defence Department had 339 on its payroll assigned to Capitol Hill. Incidentally, it would seem that high-ranking American military officers are much like Congressmen in certain respects. It is a matter of public record that in 1959 the top 100 American defence contractors had provided jobs for 721 retired staff officers, colonels and above: by 1969 the figure had risen to 2,072. Yet Senators are apt to wax indignant about conflict of interest when it arises in the Executive and Judiciary branches of government. Before they would confirm Nixon's cabinet appointments, members were most insistent that the nominees should divest themselves of their holdings in enterprises doing business with the Government. This would seem, of course, perfectly proper, but in practice no matter how many ironclad arrangements are made, such as the creation of independently administered trust funds and so on, most Americans accept that the whole thing is a charade. Just how difficult it is to remove all traces of taint is illustrated by Nixon's attempt to fill a vacancy on his US Supreme Court. His first nominee was turned down, partially on the grounds that he was revealed to have tried cases as a Federal judge involving business concerns in which he had a shareholding interest. The second was turned down largely on the grounds of his patent mediocrity. The next man he picked, it emerged, had also tried three cases as a Federal judge involving companies in which he held a few shares. The Court appointment was itself to fill a vacancy created by the resignation of Johnson's friend, Abe Fortas, following disclosures that he had accepted fees from a family charity set up by a man who was then doing time for stock market manipulation. In the whole squabble confidence in Justice and the Law was again a casualty. The erosion of confidence in the integrity of high public servants leads soon to the erosion of the principle of integrity in the nation.

Americans are beginning to have serious doubts about themselves. Those who would deny this assertion in public and for the record are often the very ones whose doubts are the deepest. The nation's leader class is on the verge of a nervous breakdown of alarming proportions. This should not be a cause for rejoicing even in Moscow and Peking, for an unstable US would in turn unsettle the delicate balance of power.

Such corruption and falsity in US is recognized by the rising generation. It is openly cynical about its own élite and alienated by the defects it perceives and feels unable to do anything effective to correct. In such a situation there cannot but be a perilous loss of that reasoned self-esteem which is an essential ingredient in any people that aspire to respect in the world: an essential ingredient, indeed, of civilized nationhood itself.

13

Polarization, Decay and Isolation

Dr Milton Eisenhower, the late President's brother and chairman of the White House Commission on the Causes and Prevention of Violence, made an observation on television recently: 'Of the twenty-one civilizations that failed, nineteen failed because of internal decay, not of external forces.' He went on to add that he was much concerned about 'the growing intellectual polarization of our society. We have to be concerned about minority groups not getting true justice. And here we are, the most affluent country in the world, and we haven't yet solved the problems of poverty and hunger—and this is leading to still deeper internal divisions. It is all these things and more that indicate to me a weakening of the whole American internal structure.'

Dr Eisenhower is worried about these things, and frustrated because Congress will do nothing to cope with such lunatic situations as that which sees 90 million guns loose in homes throughout the country, 25 million of which are pistols whose only purpose is to kill people. Compound statistics like these with *Time* magazine's recent calculation that 6 million young Americans now have taken or are taking drugs, 2 million of them being more or less dependent on them. There *is* reason to be scared. Nixon himself remarked on the fact at a meeting he called of all the 50 State Governors not long ago to discuss the drug problem that there was no record of a civilization having survived narcotic addiction. It was subsequently discovered to the embarrassment of more than one of the executive dignitaries assembled that several children in their own immediate families had been caught with marihuana.

The crumbling of American society is reflected physically in urban deterioration. The American city is in a state of galloping decay that can be identified in one case after another across the country. The cycle is quite simple: the city centre or downtown is progressively deserted by Middle Americans for suburbia. The breadwinner commutes by concrete super-highway from his antiseptic dormitory of real estate developers' standardized dream-house to and from work. Construction of that highway itself creates slums underneath it. But the suburbanite looks neither left nor right. The blight is all but invisible to him as he walks a few steps from parking lot to office block. Because he, as taxpayer, no longer lives in the city, the city fathers cannot collect much out of him. If they are to maintain essential services, not to mention stopping the rot in the inner city spreading further, they must raise funds. But if they try to levy taxes on the businesses that keep headquarters in the city still, then they will tend to drive them away altogether—a process one can see occurring already in many.

Given the tools of modern communications and computers, there is no longer any overridingly compelling reason that downtown should survive as the traditional exchange and mart. The day can be foreseen when, assuming that the institution survives it, Wall Street will become the label on a giant computer capable of performing all the functions required by borrowers, lenders, speculators and brokers. There are already large numbers of active investors who never go near

New York and who have found they can function very satisfactorily from beach houses in Florida or desert ranches in Arizona, thanks to electronics. This practice is sure to spread as the big cities progressively succumb to their cancer.

This gloomy cycle of decay could, of course, be arrested by deliberate action. But the Middle American tends to regard even the contemplation of such action as radical, visionary nonsense that will push up his taxes. His instinct is to pull back deeper—from suburbia to exurbia. With a few notable exceptions, civic pride is not marked in America for the simple reason that as a restless people Americans have shallow roots. A remarkably high proportion of them move lock-stock-and-barrel from one city to another three or four times in their lives. This is particularly true of precisely that class which might be deemed the best trained and equipped to cope with the cities' problems—the managers, technicians, scientists and engineers. That fierce sense of traditional habitat that compels the people of Hamburg, Dresden or Coventry, for example, to rebuild from ground up is absent in those who have never had such deep feelings for a special patch of earth but have regarded it as natural to use up, throw away and move on to where there is plenty more room over the next hill line. Only very recently has the realization dawned in America that this may be a suicidally wasteful procedure, and that the affluent society is in real danger from its effluent. Here again, however, such thoughts are apt to be branded 'socialistic' because they imply interference by the State.

Nothing much will be done to reverse the downward slide of the nation's cities while the war in Asia continues. This much is accepted on all sides. That Nixon has been unable thus far to extricate America from Indochina as fast as the silent majority hoped and expected is certainly the major frustration. The longer this situation drags on, the more certain is it that isolationism will grow. The strain on the national economy is already severe and it cannot be relieved without the imposition of controls—and this again would be rejected as more 'socialism'. It would be seen as a capitulation to the very evils that Middle America looked to Nixon to correct.

Similarly, unrest in America's universities is not dying down. Nor is it in the black slums. Protest assumes new forms. It is muddled, incoherent and not well-led. But sweeping it under the rug is unlikely to resolve the situation or head off further and more outrageous explosions.

The way things are going today, Bill Shirer's forecast of America's being likely to become the first country to go fascist democratically looks far more plausible than the threat of revolution from the New Left. The hippies, hopheads and the flower children are scarcely a political force—indeed they have, by definition, opted out. America's liberal intelligentsia, which has provided the luminaries of the Democratic Party ever since Franklin Roosevelt came in with his New Deal in 1933, has lost its drive and stands discredited in the eyes of the middle mass. Liberal Republicans are in nearly as bad a fix.

Should the Communists in Vietnam try and force a showdown that would compel Nixon either to face a humiliation for his remaining forces or to escalate the war once more, and should the economic picture deteriorate further on the home front, the prospect of the nation turning towards what is known as the Man on Horseback—a popular dictator—is not to be lightly dismissed. It would be a great mistake to imagine that a swing to reaction would be anything but inward-looking.

American authoritarians in the past have always tended to be rigidly isolationist. It must be assumed they would be so again, especially since, in the interest of reinflating the punctured national ego, they would clearly be inclined to hold all foreigners responsible for their unhappy condition.

The drift towards the ugly Right, which is of a mean and narrow sort and should not be confused with the conservatism known in Britain, can be detected in various areas. For example, the freedom of comment in America's leading newspapers has lately been subtly curtailed by Vice-President Spiro Agnew—and perfectly legitimately some feel. Agnew, having been angered by what he felt to be the excessive criticism of the Nixon Administration and its policies, particularly in Vietnam, pointed out in a speech that the most influential newspapers in the country were controlled by the liberal Eastern Establishment. These opinion-makers also owned magazines and television stations. Was this not a clear case of a dangerous monopoly? he asked. He further insinuated that the matter might perhaps be investigated by the Federal Communications Commission to see whether such a situation did not infringe the law by giving too much power to a single group. A shudder went through the Ivy Leaguers. And it turned to near-panic when the public opinion polls revealed that Agnew's views not only enjoyed widespread popular support but that he had become the third best-liked man in the nation—after Nixon and the evangelist Billy Graham. None of these three exactly appeal to America's upper classes. But, as if by magic, the tone of the Press and television comment about Nixon and his cabinet suddenly changed overnight. Agnew jokes began to fade from the air and print.

Agnew became the fastest rising star in the nation's

political firmament early in 1970. He was already being boosted as the ideal Mr Republican for the Presidential elections of 1976. Breaking all precedent for what had hitherto been regarded as a distinctly backseat job, he emerged as the new darling of Middle Americans alarmed by violence in the streets, by Black Panthers, by the militants of the big city slums and the preachers of revolution. He detests the liberals of gentle birth with their cultured accents who, as he sees it, are guilty of 'élitism' and 'philosophical violence' because of their tenderness towards student radicals and dissenters. The message he delivered stumping the country was grimly reminiscent. The words echoed Adolf Hitler's own, as Senator Edmund Muskie has pointed out, uttered in 1932: 'The streets of our country are in turmoil. The universities are filled with students rebelling and rioting. Communists are seeking to destroy our country. Russia is threatening us with her might and the Republic is in danger ... from within and without. We need law and order. Without it the nation cannot survive.' It all strikes a warm response among stolid suburbanites, as when he calls critics of Nixon's Vietnam policy 'impudent snobs'.

Judge William Douglas, the liberal Supreme Court justice whom Agnew-type Congressmen are keen to impeach as a dangerous radical, recently reminded his countrymen of something they would rather forget today: that they are themselves the product of a rebellion that took place nearly 200 years ago. 'George III,' he wrote, 'was the symbol against which our Founders made a revolution now considered bright and glorious, George III had not crossed the seas to fasten a foreign yoke on us. George III and his dynasty had established us and nurtured us and all that he did was by no means oppressive. But a vast restructuring of laws and institutions was necessary if the people were to be content. The restructuring was not forthcoming and there was a revolution.' Judge Douglas added: 'Today's Establishment is the new George III. Whether it will continue to adhere to his tactics, we do not know. If it does, the redress, honoured by tradition, is also revolution.'

This was taken by Middle Americans to mean that he was urging revolution. But then few had actually read his book. What he was talking about was the technological revolution and its impact. The revolution he foresees is that in which mankind must seek out ways to 'make the machine—and the vast bureaucracy of the corporation state and of the Government that runs the machine—the servant of man' rather than his master.

Nixon's constituency—the great silent majority of America—is ill-equipped mentally, emotionally and by temperament for the readjustments that are forcing themselves upon the nation. It would be wrong to characterize this numerically dominant bloc merely as a small-minded, smug and essentially selfish bourgeoisie, any more than one could say the same of its counterpart in Victorian England a century ago. But it certainly remains to be seen whether an instinctively conservative and self-brainwashed a society can produce heroes capable of the inspired leadership needed in what is plainly an era of revolutionary crisis.

For Britain and Western Europe the lesson is clear: we must make ready at once and without delay to stand on our own feet and stop leaning on the United States. We must face the hard fact that one of these days it is entirely conceivable that an isolationist, Far Right-dominated Washington will reach an accommodation with Moscow. America's attitude to Russia and China of uncompromising and frozen hostility is breaking up already, not because either side, nor any in the triangle, believes the other has undergone a change of heart. It is simply that the US is no longer so interested in championing the cause of freedom and that the USSR is frightened of China. Europe may soon be out in the cold, regarded as irrelevant in America's calculations.

We need to mark well the trends developing in the United States so as to avoid the pitfalls that beset them. We have, goodness knows, much to do to put our own house in order and expand our co-operation with our immediate neighbours and natural partners in Europe. We should certainly not indulge in any rancour. To accept the probability that America may withdraw into its shell is not to wish it to happen but to prepare to face a fact of life.

It is my contention that it has been too easy for us all —in the Old World as well as the New—to accept as somehow immutable, if not altogether right and proper, the paramountcy of American leadership. In this generation we have let ourselves be blinded by the wizardry of scientific marvels, awakening only lately to the possibility that the earth's ecological balance may have been irreparably harmed by much of it. *Savoir faire* is not necessarily as important as *savoir vivre*: technological know-how should not be confounded with Progress in all respects. It may be disturbing to discover these things but it would be outright folly not to admit them.

It could well be that American power has come a full cycle in terms of the nation's will and sense of purpose. But then it could also be that super-powers, as such, are not yet workable. The US has vast military strength and industrial capacity; so has Russia. China and India are both huge in terms of population. But the power of any or all of them is merely potential if leadership and will are lacking.

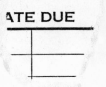